The Experience Effect

Engage Your Customers with a Consistent
and Memorable Brand Experience

Jim Joseph

⁂AMACOM
American Management Association
New York • Atlanta • Brussels • Chicago • Mexico City • San Francisco
Shanghai • Tokyo • Toronto • Washington, D.C.

This publication is designed to provide accurate and authoritative information in regard to the subject matter covered. It is sold with the understanding that the publisher is not engaged in rendering legal, accounting, or other professional service. If legal advice or other expert assistance is required, the services of a competent professional person should be sought.

Library of Congress Cataloging-in-Publication Data
Joseph, Jim, 1963–
    The experience effect : engage your customers with a consistent and memorable brand experience / Jim Joseph.
        p. cm.
    Includes bibliographical references and index.
    ISBN-13: 978-0-8144-1554-2 (hbk.)
    ISBN-10: 0-8144-1554-7 (hbk.)
    1. Branding (Marketing) 2. Brand loyalty. 3. Customer relations. I. Title.
    HF5415.1255.J67 2010
    658.8'27—dc22   2009053576

About AMA
American Management Association (www.amanet.org) is a world leader in talent development, advancing the skills of individuals to drive business success. Our mission is to support the goals of individuals and organizations through a complete range of products and services, including classroom and virtual seminars, webcasts, webinars, podcasts, conferences, corporate and government solutions, business books, and research. AMA's approach to improving performance combines experiential learning—learning through doing—with opportunities for ongoing professional growth at every step of one's career journey.

Printing number
10 9 8 7 6 5 4 3 2

*To **Christopher, Alicia, JP,** and **Sophie***
for all our experiences together.

Trademarked terms appearing in *The Experience Effect*

7-Eleven

A&E
Abercrombie & Fitch
American Express
American Heart
   Association's "Go
   Red for Women"
Arm & Hammer

Biggest Loser Club, The
BlackBerry
Britney Spears
   Curious

Calvin Klein
Campbell's
ChapStick
Chipotle Mexican Grill
ck one
Clean & Clear
Clorox (Mr. Clean)
CoverGirl

Diet Coke
Diet Pepsi
Dunkin' Donuts
Durex

eMarketer

Facebook
FUBU

Gap, The (RED)
Garnier Fructis
Gillette Mach 3 Turbo

Healthy Choice
Hershey's Bliss
Hershey's Kisses

"Intel Inside"
iPhone
iPod
iVillage.com

J.C. Penney
J.Crew

Keebler
Kellogg's Rice Krispies
Kenneth Cole
Kindle
KitchenAid
Kmart

L'Oréal
La Grenouille
Latisse
Levi's
LinkedIn
Lotrimin Ultra
Louis Vuitton

M&M's Premiums
McDonald's McCafe
Marriott Rewards
   Program
Martha Stewart Living
Martha Stewart Show,
   The
Mercedes-Benz
MySpace

Nasonex

Neutrogena
Nike ClimaFIT
Nike swoosh

Olay
Oral-B

Pillsbury
Pottery Barn
Priceline.com

Ralph Lauren
Ralph Lauren Classics
Ralph Lauren Double
   RL
Ralph Lauren Rugby
Reach
(RED)

Singulair
Southwest Airlines
Starbucks
Susan G. Komen for
   the Cure

Tide
Tim Hortons
TiVo
Trojan
Twitter
Tylenol

Verizon
Von Dutch FUBU

Wal-Mart

Yahoo

Contents

Thoughts from Two Icons

I spent the bulk of my agency career with The Publicis Groupe. It became home to the agency that I had originally created, and I ran several different agencies during my time there. The last few years I was head of Saatchi & Saatchi Wellness, where I had the opportunity to interact with some of the greatest talent in the industry. For my book, I asked two iconic legends in the advertising and marketing world to contribute their thoughts here. I hope you enjoy hearing from them.

*First is **Helayne Spivak,** a creative genius, who has run some of the most innovative creative departments on the planet. Helayne was a turning point for both the agency and me when she became the Chief Creative Officer.*

* * *

Marketing is not that difficult. Which is why it's so surprising that not many people do it well. Including those who profess to be marketers. Well, now there's no excuse. Jim Joseph's book *The Experience Effect* is a simple, clear, intelligent, personal, proven, and extremely readable book of the basic and not-so-basic marketing principles of today.

Years ago, while at a meeting, I was listening to one of my associates lay out a strategy for a new brand the agency had been assigned. After the meeting I said to him, "You know what's so brilliant about you? You're not afraid to state the obvious." Not being a humble man, but a very smart one, he responded, "No, the brilliance is in knowing what the obvious is."

Jim states the obvious: A brand must have a point of view. A look. A feel. A personality. It must be communicated consistently, but not blandly, across every consumer point of contact. Easy for him to say. And now, he's made it easy for the rest of us to learn. He brings these principles to light using everyday brands as examples of how-to and how-not-to. My personal favorite is how he compares the brand Madonna (yes, THAT Madonna) to Tide laundry detergent. Let's just say Madonna does a better job at removing stains.

In addition to relevant examples, he also gives us tangible tools such as a perceptual map, so we can see where a brand sits relative to its competition, with an action plan to put in place so we can best use the knowledge.

Whether you've just decided to pursue a career in marketing, or you're just tired of your competitor's brand doing a better job than yours, this book will be a guiding light and an awakening. I've had the advantage of being able to learn from Jim every day. Now you can share the experience.

* * *

*Now enter **Kevin Roberts,** CEO of Saatchi & Saatchi Worldwide. He is not only an inspirational leader, but an author as well. His "Lovemarks" revolutionized how marketers think about branding. I have followed Kevin with great respect and admiration. He is a force from whom we can all learn.*

*   *   *

Saatchi & Saatchi has long believed in the power of the printed word to share ideas. We've published books on Lovemarks, sisomo, world-changing ideas, social work, and leadership. Now comes a new work on marketing. Jim Joseph, who engineered Saatchi & Saatchi Wellness, has written an extremely readable and useful marketing how-to book: *The Experience Effect.*

I believe that leading brands thrive when they combine love and respect, and are founded on the fundamentals of authenticity, performance, and trust. This is where Jim's hands-on and personal approach to marketing excels.

The Experience Effect is a practical guide on how to build a consistent, compelling brand experience from touchpoint to touchpoint, a must in today's new media world. With all the brouhaha around new media and the Internet, it's easy to get caught up in the virtual craze du jour. While marketers should absolutely stay current, they must also stay steadfast in their quest to build a brand. Which means understanding the fundamentals of building their brand consistently at every touchpoint.

Jim understands this very well. He's grounded yet innovative, pragmatic yet inspired. He's an experienced marketer who has built a few Lovemarks of his own. He knows what he's doing.

Jim's sound advice and helpful tools will help any marketer, especially a seasoned one, wrestle with the ever-changing developments in the new economic reality. His approach of marketing based on fundamentals can be applied to any new challenge that pops up. Worth a read!

"Just Stick It Between Your Legs"

To me, the best part about marketing is getting to know consumers. Dissecting their lives and figuring out what motivates them is at the heart of creating a brand. Consumers should be the beginning, middle, and end of every single marketing plan, be it for a large consumer brand or for a small business.

So I asked my current partner, Maureen Lippe, Founder and CEO of Lippe Taylor Brand Communications, to share some insights about consumers. Maureen has built her career around understanding women as purchasers and influencers. If you don't understand women, then you can't possibly understand consumers. Here Maureen teaches us a little lesson to get us started.

* * *

You've made a very wise decision to invest your valuable time reading *The Experience Effect*. It is an investment that will pay off immediately. It's a must-read, a practical how-to prescription on how to build an appropriate and sustainable brand experience for your consumers consistently across an entire marketing plan. You will love it for its easy and personal style, its great examples, and its no-nonsense approach. Most important, if you are in marketing or have a product or service you want to sell, you will be able to apply the principles and use them to effectively solve your daily challenges.

All of us are trying to understand and leverage the complex world of new and newer media options these days. It seems that every brand wants to use every one of them, which requires us to follow a rigorous marketing process even more diligently to make the right decisions for the brand. *The Experience Effect* gives you a framework for both choosing among those options and then knowing what to do with them. It's a smart book for anyone in marketing or anyone trying to bring a product to market.

No surprise, it's written by Jim Joseph, a classically trained marketing professional. He's not a statistician or a professor. He's a seasoned marketer who has been in the trenches, in many arenas, on both the agency side and the client side. He's managed brands big and small, in many different kinds of organizations. He's ridden almost every new marketing wave and knows how to make good choices in his brands' plans. There are not many situations that Jim has not seen, experienced, or gotten his way out of. He started out at Johnson & Johnson where he learned the fundamentals of consumer packaged goods marketing; he has merged and reinvented big agencies in a multinational holding company; and now he's my partner at Lippe Taylor Brand Communications.

Jim is one of those marketers who really empathizes with and understands his target consumer, no matter the demographic. As marketers, most of our consumers are women—and I'm sure we've all read about the purchasing power of women. "Girls Rule"—meaning that women make the vast majority of purchase decisions about brands in our economy. If you don't understand what they want from brands and how to market to them effectively, they will "Rule You Out!" They will then tell their friends, who will tell their friends, and your brand could become history. Social media has made it all the more easy and fast. Understanding women's beliefs, values, and psychological makeup is critical to a successful brand and it's critical to building the experience effect.

In understanding consumers, particularly women, it's important to respect them, their friends, and their lives. Jim spends a lot of time talking about the importance of understanding consumers, one of my favorite parts of the book. How can you build an experience for consumers if you don't really understand them?

If you are going to maximize the brand experience, as Jim says, there are some things you need to think about when communicating to your consumers, particularly women.

First of all, authenticity is paramount. A brand needs to say what it means and mean what it says. Women value brands that have values, beyond just price. A brand that is authentic gets into the consideration set and then the consideration set of her network. One false move can turn the whole thing off.

Women are gatherers. They gather information when making a purchase decision and they seek out advice from friends and professionals they trust and from people going through the same situation. The Internet tends to be the first stop, and don't underestimate the power of her girlfriends. She meets them online, and their powerful numbers can damage a brand in thirty seconds. Jim has a good example of this later in the book. Tap into the "gatherer" mentality and join the search so that when she makes a purchase decision, your brand is already right beside her.

As much as we may share, we are all very concerned about privacy, especially online. Be caring with sensitive issues and only talk to her when invited. Don't reach out unless she's either asked you or she's ready to hear from you. And don't ever breach confidentiality or privacy. You'll be out of favor faster than it took to turn off the computer.

Once you convince a consumer to buy your product, you need to sustain that relationship. Women are very loyal, but their needs and opinions change over time as they progress through life stages. As a brand, you have to keep up and constantly add value to life's changing needs.

And most important, women generally buy based on how they feel. Yes, they gather facts. But when it comes right down to it, the purchase decision is based largely on emotions. Jim spends a lot of time making sure that the experience effect has an emotional side. The facts alone will not cut it. A woman needs to feel good about her purchase on many levels.

Here's a great story that I've heard several people tell. It's a true story, but it's almost become an urban legend in marketing. Though I can't take credit for it, it's a great lesson in understanding your consumer and the influencers on brand decisions. Here's how the story goes.

A woman walks into a car showroom (sounds like a joke but there's nothing funny about the outcome), one of those fancy foreign-car showrooms, with her husband. The salesman immediately pops up from his desk to greet the couple. He is completely focused on the husband, and gives polite recognition to the woman and a slight nod to their two kids.

The couple looks around at the cars, with salesman in tow, asking questions here and there. The husband's questions are taken very seriously, but the salesman somewhat dismisses the questions coming from the wife—this despite the fact that they are buying a car for her to use and that they have made that very clear!

Getting rather annoyed by the salesman's dismissal, she asks a question that women frequently want to know when purchasing a car, and his answer ultimately sinks the deal and many others to come: "Why aren't there any cup holders?" A logical question, quite honestly, for a woman who spends a lot of time in the car commuting to work and shuttling the kids around.

The salesman, however, doesn't get or care about the seriousness of the question. He answers back, "Cup holders? Europeans don't eat or drink in their cars! If you really need to drink in the car, why don't you just stick it between your legs."

"Just stick it between your legs!"—can you believe that retort? This is the straw that breaks the customer's back and kills the sale instantly. The woman immediately walks out the door with her kids and husband, and needless to say does not buy a car from that salesman or from that brand.

But here's the real moral to this story. Within five minutes of getting home, she updates her status online and reports about her experience, "outing" the European car manufacturer and dealership. She tells the "just stick it between your legs" story to everyone she knows, through her entire network of friends. And then they tell their friends, and so on, just like in that famous shampoo commercial from the seventies. And another brand goes on the "hit list."

That car salesman had no idea what he was doing or that he blew the sale with one outrageous remark. He had no clue how to relate to a woman because he hadn't been schooled in understanding consumers. He certainly didn't understand that women buy half of the cars sold in the United States and influence the purchase of far many more than that. So not only did he not make that sale, he also isn't going to be getting any traffic from her friends either.

The point is not that *The Experience Effect* is all about women. Quite the contrary. As marketers, we need to understand the needs of the whole family, any family, and of all our target markets, to monitor how the brand fits in their lives. Understanding consumers, female or not, is at the root of a brand's success, and it should be the beginning of any marketing initiative. Just one of the many marketing lessons you will learn in *The Experience Effect*.

Enjoy Jim's book. Happy marketing!

Acknowledgments

SPECIAL THANKS TO ALL those responsible for the defining moments of my career. We are all products of our experiences. As a career marketing professional, I am simply a product of all the incredibly talented people I have worked with through the years. It is you who have made me my own brand of marketer and leader, and it is you who have shaped my skills and my career. For that I am eternally grateful.

Mentors: Because of some incredible first job experiences, my career in marketing got off to a terrific start and has lasted a lifetime. As a teenager, my first job was at J. C. Penney, where I learned all about customer service. Then right out of college I was in sales at the Carnation Company, which led me to a path in marketing. And my first job after graduate school was at Johnson & Johnson, where I confirmed that marketing would be my career passion. I single out these first jobs as defining moments in my career because it was my first bosses and mentors there who molded and shaped me the most as a professional, as a marketer, and, dare I say, as an adult. Through the years I have been so fortunate to work with one great boss after another, right up to this moment. To each and every one of you, thanks for your support, guidance, knowledge, and trust. Every moment has counted and all moments have led to this book—something that I've dreamed of since my first day on the job.

Teammates: More so than in any other industry, any marketer is only as good as the teammates surrounding him. I have had the privilege of working with the best in the business, just as much now as ever. It's been an honor watching you all create such meaningful work, and I'd like to thank you for allowing me to be a part of your career. There's at least one moment a day where we shine, and it's because we work so well together.

Colleagues: All around the industry I have made wonderful friendships—it is the one big benefit of the profession. Having the luxury of grabbing a drink at the end of the day to bounce an idea off a colleague and friend is truly a joy. Thanks for all the glasses of white wine and "therapy" sessions through the years.

Clients: When I first made the switch to the agency side, so many people asked me how I was going to deal with being pushed around by all those difficult clients. I love it! The truth is that I've learned so much from every client. The opportunity to work on so many diverse businesses at any given moment is such a gift. It's been a pleasure helping you guide your businesses through a range of marketing challenges—big and small.

Family and Friends: Although it doesn't always seem this way, I don't live to work. I work for my family and friends. The moments with you are all the reason I need to get up every morning. I live for you and thank you for all the love you've shown. Literally, I couldn't do it without you.

Marketing Is a Spectator Sport

Observing, Learning, and Then Applying

WE INTERACT WITH BRANDS ALL THE TIME, whether we consciously realize it or not. Some brands we've been loyal to for years (like a favorite shampoo or pair of jeans), and some we are just discovering for the very first time (like a new enhanced water drink or a new electronic device). Some we don't even know are brands (like our favorite singer or a local restaurant)! Our interactions can run the gamut from amazing to just okay to disappointing to completely horrible.

Like clicking on a banner ad that takes you to a website where you find the perfect item you didn't even realize you wanted, in a cool color you didn't even realize existed, and discovering that it comes with free shipping—coincidently only on orders placed that day! Pretty amazing. Or stopping at your favorite coffee shop, noticing that it's a lot messier than it used to be, getting the wrong flavor added to your usual coffee drink, and then being charged 67 cents more than usual. Very disappointing.

These kinds of interactions are our personal experiences with brands, and they completely shape our perceptions. They influence our feelings about the brand, good or bad, whether we realize it or not. These experiences define our thoughts, attitudes, and behaviors toward brands and the value that they bring to our lives.

In a sense, how we experience the brand, how we feel the brand, and how we choose to interpret the brand actually becomes the brand to us. This is *The Experience Effect,* and throughout the book we'll be exploring the effect that brand experiences have on consumers.

At the crux of good marketing is the conscious and methodical process of determining exactly the kind of brand to offer consumers and exactly the kind of experience to create for them—and then developing it consistently across every facet of the marketing plan: from obvious marketing elements like packaging and advertising, to the not so obvious elements like customer service representatives, the CEO's weekly blog, or a branded Twitter presence. The essence of good marketing is creating a consistent brand experience with each specific consumer interaction.

In *The Experience Effect,* I will walk you through that conscious and methodical process step by step, chapter by chapter. By the end, we will have mapped out a consistent and ownable brand experience for the entire marketing plan.

We will also be exploring a lot of examples here. Some of the examples will be personal, and some observational. Some we'll explore in depth, and others will be brief mentions to help make a point. I love looking at and analyzing examples of good and bad marketing, and you'll get a load of them in this book. Marketplace examples help bring to life the principles of marketing that are otherwise left to theory. When we observe marketing theory applied in the real world to real brands, we can learn from both the successes and mistakes of others and apply what we've learned to our own marketing challenges.

In this book we'll look at brands from sportswear to restaurants and from cookies to celebrities. We'll look at traditional, digital, and social media forms of communication. Some examples will be real brands that have become a part of pop cul-

> *Marketing is a spectator sport and we can all learn by watching brands in action!*

ture, and other examples will remain unbranded to help make a point more clearly. We can learn something a little different from each one of them. My hope is to bring the principles of the experience effect to life through these examples. Marketing is a spectator sport and we all can learn by watching brands in action!

My goal in writing was to make this book easy to read. There'll be no heavy technical jargon or complicated theories, no buzzwords or three-dimensional spreadsheets, just some practical advice with a real-world approach. In many cases, I'll simplify a concept we're discussing just to make the point clearer. It's kind of my style in life. It's not that I don't want to present the complexity of the concepts; it's just that I believe that simplicity brings clarity. We can always add complexity later.

Here's how *The Experience Effect* will unfold. First we'll talk about what it is and why it's important, and then we will build it together. Step by step.

In chapter one, we'll do a full-scale definition of "the experience effect" so we can all start out on the same page, so to speak. Like I said, no buzzwords and technical jargon, just a real-life definition that we can wrap our heads around.

In chapter two we'll outline the importance of brand experiences to successful marketing. I'm hoping that it has already started to prove its worth. Chapter two is where you'll get the answer to the question "Why bother?".

In chapter three we'll take the first step toward leveraging the experience effect by defining the brand. We need to know the brand intimately before starting to build a consumer experience for it. We need to make some conscious decisions up front to guide the brand definition process and to make sure that the experiences come out the way we intend, including putting a stake in the ground about the brand and its offerings for consumers. To help clarify the brand definition, we will compare and contrast it using other brands within the same category.

Chapters four, five, and six are devoted to consumer targeting. Good marketing begins and ends with consumers, so we'll take a look at understanding our consumer targets, whether a brand has one or many. We'll look at developing profiles for our consumers and how to connect with them in multiple ways. We'll explore some grassroots, real-world research techniques that will culminate in meaningful, thorough consumer understanding. Having a true understanding of the real consumer is the key ingredient in developing a brand experience.

The next three chapters, seven, eight, and nine, are where we begin constructing the foundation of the experience effect by mapping, activating, and tailoring touchpoints. As you'll see, touchpoints are so critical to the success of the brand experience and in many ways constitute the marketing plan. These days every brand is asking how to go digital and how to get into social media. By the time we're done with chapter nine, you'll know the ins and outs of maximizing touchpoints, digital and otherwise, and you'll have the knowledge necessary to tailor each relevant touchpoint for its best use.

With our plan almost completely built, chapter ten provides inspiration by looking at the best of the best in brand experiences at touchpoints. In this chapter we'll meet some of the industry's greats and see how they use touchpoints to build unique consumer interactions as part of their brand.

Chapter eleven is about making choices, and we'll take an entertaining look at celebrity brands and how they too have an experience effect. As marketers, we can learn a lot from celebrities and how they make choices to market their brands.

In chapter twelve, we'll go back to research and discover how to make sure that the touchpoint experiences we have created are effective. Each should be maximized for its best use, and research can help prove our work one way or the other. This is a well-known step in television advertising development, but we need to do the same level of due diligence for all the other touchpoints.

In chapter thirteen, it's time to make sure the brand experience is ownable, so we'll investigate ways to make sure it belongs to your brand and your brand alone. There are some simple techniques like using colors and logos, as well as more complicated ones like employing claims and brand character. We'll discuss a range of ways to make the experience effect ownable, and, of course, we'll be looking at a lot of examples.

Chapter fourteen is where we complete our work by making sure that we've fully covered all bases. We'll take a step back to see the progress we have made since the beginning of this book. You'll learn how to do a gap assessment to see what aspects need further development and to help prioritize your resources. The gap assessment also helps us to continually evolve the brand experience over time.

Marketers never act alone, so chapter fifteen will offer some tips to keep teammates in the loop and to share the full range of marketing work with everyone who touches the brand. Marketing is not only a spectator sport, but a team sport as well!

We will be building the experience effect throughout this book, from the ground up. As you read, you'll see how to create a unique brand experience in a logical, methodical fashion. Real marketplace examples will help you make it come to life.

My goal for this book is to make it not only easy to read, but also easy to apply to your own brand so that you don't just get theory, you get practicality, and so you don't just read, you apply.

The experience doesn't have to end here. Visit my website, JimJosephExp.com, to continue the journey. You can ask me questions and do some more exploring, and maybe even hook up with other marketers to compare notes.

Let the journey begin!

The Experience Effect in Action
Two Personal Examples

BEFORE WE DELVE INTO exactly what it takes to create a consistent brand experience for the consumer, let me demonstrate, in detail, how the *experience effect* plays out with two personal examples about my own interactions with J.Crew and Starbucks.

J.Crew is the comfortable, contemporary brand of preppy clothes featured in a range of wearable styles, bold colors, and geometric patterns. The J.Crew catalogs are filled with thin, young models who look amazingly comfortable in fitted, well-coordinated outfits. They look gorgeous, carefree, and alive, but not too overly styled or unattainable, just like how I want to feel. Flipping through the pages is a casual journey through the fashion season, whether it's spring, summer, winter, or fall.

The website works totally in conjunction with the catalog, exuding the same brand character. Because I am familiar with the catalog, I don't have to waste time figuring out how to find something on the website. Both venues use the same branding elements (like colors, fonts, and imagery), and both venues are structured and organized in a parallel manner. It's a comfortable experience for me in either venue, as I believe it would be even for a first-time customer.

While the website certainly allows for browsing, it is designed for easy ordering, just like the catalog. I can immediately go to the section for men and navigate by clothing type. If I want a little advice, then a style consultant will assist me—explaining, for example, the difference between a sport coat and a blazer, if that's something I need to know. New items are at the top of the navigation for frequent shoppers like me, and there's also a section for items under $100 called "Instant Gratification." "The Always List" is a particularly great feature because it showcases all the must-haves for the season, organized for men who don't like to browse or spend too much time shopping, or for women who are confused what to buy for their men.

When I know what I want I can find it quickly and proceed to checkout, and still add an extra item or two on my way. Since I am a returning customer, I can quickly follow the same pattern on every visit to the site because it is familiar and comfortable, just like the clothes. I simply click on "My Account"—and then not only can I proceed to checkout faster, but I can also see what I've ordered in the past.

The stores are totally coordinated as well. Stepping into a J.Crew store is like stepping into the catalog. All the same branding elements are in play—colors, signage, and merchandising. Selecting clothes in the store is similar to shopping on the website because everything is separated by gender and organized by type. All the khaki pants are beautifully merchandised together in one part of the store and the boxer shorts in yet another part of the store, just like the separate sections of the catalog and the navigation on the website.

There is an infectious hustle-bustle energy that makes me feel like I've been missing something all this time. I can see the clothes in action right on the salespeople, and I can feel how they might look on me. I learned a casual way to tie a tie from one of the sales associates, which was also featured on the website. The service is cautiously attentive, allowing me to browse when I want to browse or get service quickly when I am in a hurry. Of course I always think I'm in a hurry, but at J.Crew somehow I always find time to browse. During the holidays at peak shopping hours, the sales associates sometimes give out bottled water to customers waiting in line.

The new experimental concept store for men, Liquor Store, is completely geared toward the J.Crew male devotee yet located in an entirely separate location. Aimed at a more mature, more sophisticated male shopper, it features the best of the best menswear, carefully selected and merchandised to feel like it's exclusive merchandise, hand-selected for more discriminating customers. In reality, the store is full of Levi's jeans and oxford shirts sold at the same prices as in the regular store, but it feels so much more exclusive. Of course, Liquor Store is also a prominent section of the J.Crew website, a boutique concept within the main site.

Liquor Store still feels like J.Crew, but with a more exclusive edge. The first time I stepped into Liquor Store I could tell it was J.Crew even though I didn't see a J.Crew sign. Sure, the logo was similar in look, as were the clothes, but it was something more. The look and tone of the store and the way the clothes were merchandised just "felt" like J.Crew. It was an emotional reaction of feeling comfortable and familiar, and I could just tell where I was. That's the sign of the experience effect in action.

The J.Crew brand fulfills my personal needs, but it doesn't necessarily work for everyone, and that's the way good marketing works; a strong, consistent brand experience won't appeal to everyone because it needs to be specifically created for a certain target audience. I have friends who have never set foot in a J.Crew store or experienced any part of the brand, and probably never will because they have other clothing brands that better relate to them. Like the more formal feel of Banana Republic or the bolder look of Tommy Hilfiger.

I get a lot out of my interactions with J.Crew from the store, catalog, and website. I only buy the clothes I like, but I enjoy the browsing experience regardless because it gives me a mental break from my hectic routine. It's a brand I have brought into my life because it adds value to my lifestyle. Most of the time I don't consciously process it that way, but I certainly do appreciate the value the brand gives to me. My personal experience with J.Crew could be typical of any consumer's experience with a favorite brand.

To further demonstrate the experience effect, let's take a look at an example on the other end of the spectrum: my personal experience at an establishment most people know—Starbucks. While my J.Crew experiences are always consistently good regardless of the venue or time of year, I can't say the same about another brand in my life, Starbucks.

Don't get me wrong, I love Starbucks. It's another one of only a few brands that has completely infiltrated my life, no matter where I am. Every list of New Year's resolutions includes cutting back on my Starbucks habit, but I just can't seem to do it. I frequent the same three or four locations depending on my commute to work or my weekend schedule. Plus I always go to Starbucks when I'm traveling on business. It gives me a sense of familiarity and comfort no matter where I am.

When Starbucks first burst into just about every neighborhood in America, it offered a special and consistent brand experience, drink to drink and location to location. But something has changed—the experience has now become a bit of a crapshoot. And my impression of the brand has changed as a result.

In the beginning of the brand's explosion, I totally bought into the Starbucks lifestyle. I was one of the first consumers to branch out with the brand and try the new pastries, new coffee drinks, new gift items, and even the music. I loved stopping into the shop, smelling the great roasting coffee, and getting a handmade cup of customized specialized coffee, so I incorporated Starbucks into my daily routine. I even bought gift sets for my friends and family who were not necessarily Starbucks consumers. I was so aligned with the brand and the special brand experience that I wanted to extend it into other parts of my life. I would visit the website, and I often used the store locator feature when I was traveling out of town. I started to buy the coffee in the grocery store to serve at home, and I always got the Christmas blend for the holidays. I even tried the ice cream.

Slowly but surely, though, the Starbucks experience became more and more erratic and inconsistent for me, and I started to question my brand choice. The great smell of roasting coffee gave way to long lines and messy counters. The gift items looked more and more generic and the pastries started tasting less fresh. Some stores were a good brand experience, some were mediocre, and some were awful. I could never be sure of what I was going to get, and I started questioning my purchase decision. There are days when my venti skinny vanilla latte is completely satisfying and prepares me for the day ahead, and then there are days when I wonder why I continue to waste my time and money. Even worse, my favorite drink tastes different from location to location, and even costs a different amount from location to location—sometimes within the same geographic area! Makes no sense to me.

The environment in some of the stores is cozy and welcoming, and in some it is noisy and dirty. Some of the baristas are wonderfully talented and service-oriented (like the one in Greenwich Village in New York City who remembers my order every morning at 7:45 a.m.), and some act like they can't be bothered. The service has become remarkably erratic. Why should I go out of my way each day to spend more than six dollars for, let's face it, a cup of coffee and a scone, when I'm not really sure if it's going to be any good?

I stopped trying the new drinks, stopped buying the gift items, and stopped going more than once a day. I have not logged on to the website in a long time. Granted, I still frequent the stores, but my experiences are shaping my attitudes about Starbucks, and I find my consumption behavior changing as well. I'm beginning to try other options more often, simply because I don't always trust the Starbucks experience. And I don't think I'm alone.

With the erosion of the Starbucks brand, the company has invited unwelcome scrutiny of its practices (for example, the perceived high pricing) and opened the door for other brands to create a more meaningful experience for coffee drinkers. McDonald's has created McCafe as a lower cost yet still consistently high-quality alternative. Dunkin' Donuts has been extremely aggressive in communicating both the pricing and the quality of its offerings to combat Starbucks. And a brand from Canada, Tim Hortons, has also entered the U.S. market, with a just-added high-profile location in New York's Penn Station commuter train station. The inconsistency and high pricing at Starbucks have clearly opened the door for new category entrants.

As a marketer, don't ever create opportunities for competitors or reasons for loyal consumers to experiment with other options. In fact, as marketers we want to do just the opposite: uniquely fulfill consumer needs so that there's no reason for them to look elsewhere.

I offer these two examples as a way to illustrate the experience effect in action. Many argue that Starbucks has lost its unique personality, and my own inconsistent experiences are making me lose my faith in the brand. But not at J.Crew. The J.Crew experience is always characteristically consistent and unique. Now it's time to dive in.

CHAPTER 1

Buzzwords Need Not Apply
Defining the Experience Effect

LET'S START OUT BY defining the experience effect. How consumers feel about brands is completely shaped by the interactons they have with them. As we define the meaning, think of your own experiences with brands you have incorporated into your life. That will help us to create a meaningful, practical definition to guide the process

If we consciously analyze our own experiences with brands in our lives, we'll witness the experience effect in real time, both positively and negatively. I'm sure if you stop and think about it, you could easily pick a few of your favorite or not-so-favorite brands that you interact with on a regular basis and break down your feelings about them. Maybe it's a luxurious skin cream or the car you love driving. Or the brand that you keep saying you'll never buy again yet somehow find back in your life again and again, much like my own experience with Starbucks, which I discussed in the Prologue.

I have to admit that I hate business definitions because they are always so theoretical. Like the classic one that comes up in job interviews all the time: Define leadership and explain how it is different from management. Only a professor could possibly answer that off the cuff! Show me a good leader who also has great management qualities and there's the definition—live and in person. It's the same with marketing. You've probably read a bunch of definitions for marketing in your time, many of which are filled with buzzwords.

I've known several great businesspeople who can't seem to talk about marketing unless they are using buzzwords. They string them along in sentences that end up all over the place. Something like: "Let us all gain alignment around the deliverables set forth in the action standards that the sponsor presented to the steering committee for the integrated marketing initiative that will require full collaboration from all key constituents."

No buzzwords here. Just plain English.

> *When marketing is done well, the product becomes a brand.*

For me, the definition of marketing is simple: creating demand for a product or service by fulfilling a specific need for consumers in a way no one else can. When marketing is done well, the product becomes a brand.

Fortunes and careers have been made on developing a decisive strategy, breakthrough creativity, and effective media selection for brands. The direction of the brand, the creative look of the brand, the messaging, and how and where to connect with consumers in their busy lives—these are the areas where marketers need logical advice and a thorough process to accomplish their goals. Marketers need these elements to build an experience effect.

So when I am asked to define the experience effect, here's what I say:

- The "experience" is the connection the brand makes with consumers. It should be unique and consistent each time.

- The "effect" is the impact those consistent brand experiences have on consumers' lives. The impact should add value.

The experience effect connects the expressions of the brand together across all the elements of the marketing plan, over periods of time. It can be linear and follow a straight and narrow path where every single interaction is essentially the same, which may indeed make perfect sense for a brand.

This linearity is what McDonald's certainly strives for from location to location and from item to item. From the start of the brand, the advertising and promotion have aimed for this. Linear means entirely consistent from element to element, exactly what consumers would expect from McDonald's.

Or maybe not. For McDonald's the brand experience is not quite as linear as the company thinks. The advertising and the website are similar to each other, but they are completely different from most of the restaurants. I believe that the advertising sets up a certain expectation about the restaurants that they just do not deliver. The website too depicts an experience that is very different from that of the restaurants, at least the ones that I've been in lately. The advertising and the website portray a clean, friendly, wholesome place where happy children dip apples into a healthy sauce while Mom sits across an immaculate table munching on a garden-fresh salad in a clean environment where people are genuinely interacting with each other. Not to get cynical here, but that has not been my experience in the "real" restaurants, which are often dirty, unfriendly, and anything but wholesome. While the food is certainly consistent from location to location, it doesn't stack up to the beautiful and healthy imagery shown on the website and in the advertising.

Now McDonald's has done an amazing job revamping the menu to appeal to both kids and their parents (particularly with new salad options, McCafe premium coffees, and healthier options in the Happy Meals), but I would maintain that the brand experience in the restaurants is not consistent with that in other parts of the marketing mix, so much so that it's hard to imagine that it's the same brand. The food and the service portrayed in the advertising and on the website look like one brand of McDonald's, while my less-than-ideal experiences in the restaurants look like another brand of McDonald's. But there should be only one consistent brand experience.

Check out the synergy between the McDonald's restaurants and their website versus that of Chipotle Mexican Grill restaurants and their website.

Just to illustrate the point, check out the synergy between the McDonald's restaurants and their website versus that of Chipotle Mexican Grill restaurants and their website. Chipotle Mexican Grill restaurants are clean and simple, with clearly stated menus that guide consumers through the food selection process. The website has the same feel, but is loaded with information. In addition to compelling content such as videos, desktop reminders, screen savers, and ingredient information, the Chipotle Mexican Grill website also has a data-capture mechanism to build relationships with consumers who frequent the restaurant. The brand captures this data either directly from the website or from click-throughs from search engines. This is excellent marketing and a great vehicle to extend the brand experience, completely consistent with the healthy food choices and clean environments of the restaurants.

By registering on the Chipotle Mexican Grill site, loyal consumers can save time by preordering and prepaying for food to either pick up or eat in the restaurants. They can also save their menu favorites to make ordering even easier next time, either through the website or through an iPhone app. The food menus and photography are exactly as they appear in the restaurants, so there is clearly a consistent experience from website to restaurant, much more so than with McDonald's. Of course the content is all provided with a unique Chipotle Mexican Grill brand tone and character, making for entertaining navigation while exploring the brand. You can even watch a video of avocados ripening, which is consistent with the delicious guacamole in the restaurants and with the brand personality.

While some brand experiences like McDonald's attempt to be linear across marketing elements, others are more fluid, with deliberate twists and turns. These brands offer more of a spectrum of experiences with their marketing mix. Some interactions create an experience that is deeper or more robust, while other interactions are planned to be relatively superficial and quick for the consumer. There's nothing wrong with that, as long as it's intentional and coming from the same brand. It's actually smart marketing. For Chipotle Mexican Grill, the iPhone app is meant to be quick and easy, while the website is meant to be filled with a variety of rich and extended experiences. Yet they are both within the same brand character.

A simple example of the fluid type would be a brand that uses television advertising merely to create brand awareness and to drive traffic to a website where consumers can then find more detailed product information. The interactions have two totally different goals and create two different experiences, yet they are both from the same brand. Healthcare marketers use this type of approach as standard practice because the information they distribute is far too complicated for a television advertising campaign to deliver. It's technically impossible and fiscally inefficient to fit all the proper information within the constraints of the television advertising format. So healthcare marketers often use television advertising to create awareness and to redirect consumers to a website, where the brand then completes the experience with detailed information.

Mapping consistent yet tailored brand experiences is in fact creating the experience effect, whether it's online, offline, or at retail—all points within the marketing mix. It's consciously mapped out to work together, building deliberate interactions along the way, like a puzzle that wonderfully fits together from the obvious marketing elements like the advertising or the website to the less obvious elements like the company receptionist or a Facebook page.

I've worked on a number of brands across a broad range of consumer categories from prescription and over-the-counter drugs, to food, hospitality, automotive, financial services, beauty, and retail (both online and offline). I've also worked across virtually every consumer segment from babies and young kids to teens, seniors, moms, and dads; from rural to urban to domestic, international, male, female, straight, and gay. And I've also seen—in focus groups, quantitative research, and in the marketplace—the differences between generations, genders, and regions of the country. The many nuances within categories and among consumer targets are what make marketing so challenging, frustrating, fascinating, and rewarding, all at the same time.

On my brand assignments through the years, we would always follow a very rigorous process to consciously decide how we wanted to build a brand experience for consumers in every marketing venue, whether it was a promotion for Kellogg's cereal that would appear both in store and on the package, a website for AFLAC to augment the television advertising, packaging for a Reach toothbrush, or a print campaign on the many uses of Arm & Hammer baking soda. We might use television advertising to create brand equity, to communicate a core set of benefits, or to drive traffic to a website (a strategy certainly not exclusive to healthcare). The website might deliver deeper educational information, entertain, or connect consumers together through chat rooms, blogs, or message boards. The retail environment could be used to ease the purchase decision or to close the sale. And the packaging could be used to continue the experience at home. Follow-up customer service either live or online may further help to avoid any buyer's regret, when it makes sense for the brand. When appropriate, we would use online social media to get even more imbedded in consumers' lives, on their terms and with each other.

Each time and with each marketing vehicle, we consciously build a positive experience with the same brand equity and same brand voice at every occasion, yet tailored to fit that vehicle. There we go, a perfect definition of the experience effect. And I didn't even have to quote a dictionary!

It's time for a real-world example to bring our definition home.

Disney. I hesitate to use Disney only because the brand is so often showcased when talking about marketing. The truth is, though, when talking about the experience effect it is hard to find a better example. I might even go so far as to say that the Disney experience is the perfect example. Disney is a mixture of youthfulness, magic, entertainment, escapism, and fantasy, all uniquely Disney. The Disney brand is far-reaching, extending from the theme parks (obviously) to movies, television shows, merchandise, live entertainment, music, hospitality, the Internet, and travel. The source of all these is one magical place, Mickey Mouse and the Magic Kingdom, but they reach way beyond a single entity to literally dominate a child's world, right from birth and, as they say, for children of all ages.

As a marketer, part of the magic is in the incredible consistency. No matter which Disney venue, the consumer lives the true Disney experience. Cruise ships, at-home DVDs, music CDs, websites, hotels, restaurants, retail stores; it is different each time, but all of it is always Disney.

> *This is what great marketing is all about—turning a standard product that could be available anywhere into an incredible and ownable brand experience.*

Start at the website and witness how the Disney experience unfolds as it flows to retail or to a children's movie or to the vacation planner. The magic is also in how consumers interact with the products. Disney products are so much more than just the products alone; they are the Disney brand experience. As I said, this is what great marketing is all about—turning a standard product that could be available anywhere into an incredible and ownable brand experience. A Disney T-shirt is so much more than just a piece of clothing to a little girl. It's a magical way for that little girl to transform herself into a princess for a day. No other T-shirt in the world can have quite that same result because of the Disney experience effect. It is truly an ownable brand experience.

A Disney hotel is not just a place to sleep at night while on vacation with the kids; it is the magic of being on a fantastical vacation and spending the kind of quality family time that never seems to happen the rest of the year.

The Disney Store is so much more than just a retail outlet where consumers can buy play clothes, toys, and costumes for the kids. It's a fantastical escape to a magical land, conveniently located at the local mall, or magically situated on New York's Fifth Avenue or Chicago's Miracle Mile. It's an easy field trip that keeps the kids occupied while the parents get some shopping done.

Every Disney venue is also just a little bit different. It's not the exact same experience every single time. It transforms from element to element and has evolved over the years, yet it is still uniquely Disney. As consumers age and grow, the Disney experience evolves at the various venues for various ages, from princess videos to children's television programming to entertainment for preteens, teens, and even for parents. The Disney Channel is not just for toddlers. Many of the television shows and movies shown at night appeal to teenagers, and there's also a part of Disney World called Pleasure Island where adults can go and party. Completely different experiences are available for consumers as they age and as their entertainment needs change, but they are all uniquely Disney. And all of it is available on demand and even on Twitter.

Every single employee, particularly at the theme parks, is trained to embody the Disney experience and to deliver it to customers consistently every single day, no matter the Disney venue. I have not even mentioned the number of Disney marketing partnerships across a range of categories—Disney characters on cereal boxes, cookies, crackers, and other food products. These partnerships offer a magical extension of the Disney experience to other family brands as well. I created a few Disney promotional partnerships when doing work for Kellogg's cereals, and we were thrilled to leverage the Disney experience effect. Free toys from the movie *Cars* in specially marked packages, for example, complete with large in-store displays were specifically designed to sell Kellogg's cereals this way.

The Disney experience is quite inspirational but can also be very hard to live up to. Employees who don't deliver on it don't stay in customer service very long, and they probably don't stay at the company either.

Now consider another example that might be closer to the challenges facing a more "ordinary" brand. As an example, let's look at the experience effect of a small brand in a highly competitive market: skin cream. Any given brand of skin cream is so much more than just the product alone. It could be said that it is hope in a bottle, the hope of looking younger, fresher, more beautiful—hence the skin cream's premium packaging, fresh fragrance, silky texture, light color, and even its high price. The experience of using the skin cream and all its wonderful product attributes allows a woman to see and feel a difference on her face—fewer wrinkles, a clearer complexion, and softer skin. And as a result, the brand also allows a woman to freely feel all the emotions of feeling younger, fresher, and maybe even more beautiful. If the experience delivers on these promises and if the skin cream even remotely works on some level, then a woman truly does look and feel the brand's experience. The skin cream has become a brand in her eyes, and she incorporates it into her life as she sees fit. She may even become a "fan" on Facebook. It is marketing magic, perhaps not on the Disney level, but effective marketing nonetheless—all part of the experience effect.

But if the skin cream delivers on the brand promise in only some respects, then she may not believe in the brand wholeheartedly. If the packaging is beautiful but the fragrance smells musty, then how could the skin cream possibly deliver on its promise of beautiful, youthful skin? If it is merchandised poorly at retail, how can a woman justify paying a premium price?

By being purposefully consistent from marketing element to marketing element, any brand can approach the magic of Disney, even a small skin cream in a highly competitive category.

> *By being purposefully consistent from marketing element to marketing element, any brand can approach the magic of Disney.*

The essence of the experience effect is creating a continuous experience that defines the brand, an experience consumers can see, smell, and touch in every way, an experience that delivers so much more than just the product alone, an experience that turns the product into a brand, no matter when, where, or how often consumers interact with it.

Disney does this so well that no other entertainment brand can compare. That little brand of skin cream can do it too, if it makes sure that all elements are consistent with the promise of feeling younger, fresher, and more beautiful.

The Gillette brand is another great example of the experience effect. Gillette now offers a full line of men's personal care products, fulfilling almost every grooming need for men, firmly rooted in the brand's heritage of shaving. The brand has expanded greatly over time, from razors to shaving creams to deodorants to body washes to shampoos to moisturizers—all parts of a man's grooming routine. As a consumer you know exactly what you are going to get from the brand. The products are consistent, and so are the marketing experiences. From the packaging to the advertising to the websites to the customer service representatives at the company headquarters, it's all completely consistent. Each product is obviously different (it's hard for a razor to be like a skin lotion), but they all have the Gillette look and feel, and the same kind of "manly" fragrance across all products. Each element of the marketing is different as well (the advertising is maximized for television, and the various brand websites are each maximized for the online experience in each category), but they all have the same consistent Gillette experience.

As a consumer, you know it's the Gillette brand because of the unique, masculine feel of the colors, the imagery, and the tonality of the content. This is stuff for men—simple, bold, and not too expensive. Each brand experience portrays men in the same manner, cleanly groomed yet completely obtainable, beautiful male models who look like the guy next door and are chosen to impress women yet not intimidate men. Of course the products are still predominantly purchased by women, for the men in their lives.

Gillette and Disney. Perfect examples of the experience effect, and two great ways to define the concept.

As we move chapter by chapter through this book, we will methodically learn the key ingredients of effective marketing, and we will look at a lot of examples like Gillette. We won't end up with just a theoretical definition of marketing, nor of the experience effect for that matter. In fact, by the time you've finished the book, you will pragmatically understand not only the concept, but also how to build it for your brand.

CHAPTER 2

Best Pasta in Town
Positioning the Experience Effect

NOW THAT WE KNOW how to define the experience effect, why is it so important? The answer is quite simple: At its core, the experience effect becomes the brand in consumers' minds. There's no way around it. As consumers experience a brand day in and day out, their interactions become the brand to them, as they know it. Their personal experiences position the brand in their minds. It becomes much less about the facts of the product itself and more about the way consumers experience the brand. If the interactions are positive and enjoyable, then the brand is positive and enjoyable. If the interactions are frustrating and painful, then so too is the brand frustrating and painful, regardless of the product claims.

Because experiences are built from many interactions over time, it's vitally important that they be consistent and purposeful each time.

In essence, these experiences define the brand and position it in consumers' minds, which makes or breaks its success. Because experiences are built from many interactions over time, it's vitally important that they be consistent and purposeful each time. Otherwise, consumers will not really know what the brand is all about and will not know how it can add value to their lives. Or what was once a positive and enjoyable brand becomes frustrating and painful.

A personal example might help make the point. I had a favorite Italian restaurant in New York that I used to go to all the time. This little place had the very best spaghetti and meatballs that I have ever had. It's dimly lit and cozy, in a real welcoming space. It's so inexpensive that it's hard to believe that it's actually in New York. Locals would go there looking for real authentic food, without the hype of the high-end culinary establishments filled with tourists and businesspeople. It was a hidden secret, a little escape. I would never go to this little Italian gem with a big crowd and I certainly didn't go there to get gourmet food. I would never go there on a date with someone that I didn't know really well, although I can't specifically say why. I'd never take a client there. Instead, I would go there with one or two good friends to get authentic Italian food in an environment that allowed us to laugh out loud and enjoy each other's company.

There were no Jimmy Choo high heels in this joint. But there were red and white checkered tablecloths, candles stuck in Chianti bottles, and the best marinara sauce I have ever had. You could bring your own bottle of wine to go with a big bowl of pasta, just $11.99! I always got a huge fresh-cut salad, served with the tangiest balsamic vinegar dressing in the city. The same waitstaff greeted me every night with big hugs and kisses every time I walked in the door. It doesn't get any better than that, especially on a Sunday night!

I had been going to this restaurant for years, loving every experience. I hadn't realized it, but evidently the long-term owners sold the restaurant to one of the head chefs. No problem, since he was the guy making all this incredible food anyway. I hadn't even realized that it had happened, which is just the way I like it; I went there for the food, not the drama. But the only reason I knew something had happened was because I noticed the menu was changing. Not the regular menu, because all the favorites were there, still as good as ever and still at the same price. But the chef, now the executive chef, had added specials each night that showed off his culinary expertise, taking me completely by surprise. Appetizers like escargot and fois gras and entrées like duck and rare tuna steaks started to appear, at close to $30.00, still served on the same dishes with the same red and white checkered tablecloths. And the menu was still written by hand on the same chalkboards, hung on the same (oddly stained) walls.

I never ordered any of these specials, and I don't think anyone ever ordered them, as far as I could tell. These specials just started appearing out of the blue, and I don't think any of the regulars cared. Clearly, these new appetizers and entrées were a major disconnect for the restaurant's customers, patrons like me who were consistently coming to this restaurant because we wanted the specific experience we had come to know and love. We frequented the restaurant because of the way we had positioned it in our minds. That very special, specific experience, for us, had become the brand. It was what the restaurant was all about. Everything about the brand was consistent, from the food, to the atmosphere, to the menu, to the waitstaff, to the prices. As a consumer I had

made a decision to include it in my life, and that's why I frequented the place so much.

The executive chef wanted something different. So he started
making changes when he really didn't understand what his restaurant brand was all about and what his customers wanted. His idea
of the brand was different from his customers' perceptions and
desires, which might be okay in some cases, but it can be a very
slippery marketing slope to be sure.

Here's where it all took a turn for the bad. Over time, as the
chef's specialties kept sitting there unsold, he seemed to grow
resentful. And so did his waitstaff, which was such a big part of the
restaurant experience. Many of the regulars started comparing
notes and commented that no one seemed excited to see us anymore. The place was changing and we didn't know why and we
certainly didn't have a say. The entire essence of the restaurant
was changing, and no one was happy about it. Who wants to work
at a restaurant where the customers are no longer happy? Who
wants to work at a restaurant that might not be making money
anymore?

Now change can be good, and I am a proponent of continually evolving as a brand. As marketers we need to evolve and keep
up with changing consumer needs and wants. But when the brand
experience radically changes and inconsistency becomes the
norm, it's often not good for business. When the brand evolution
is not in sync with the brand's consumers, then it's not generally
for the positive, unless, of course, a new set of consumers is building the business in return.

Then I noticed that the food started suffering. The pasta sauce
just wasn't the same. Between the wait staff and the food, the
brand was diminishing right before my eyes. Everything I thought
defined the brand for me was disappearing, with nothing to

replace it that made sense to me as a customer. I honestly don't know what happened, so I can't finish the story; I have not been back in over a year. My bet is that many others have abandoned the brand as well.

The sad part is that the restaurant had become more than just a place to get food for me; it had become an experience that uniquely fulfilled a need. I needed a place I could call my own, where I could walk in and be treated like family, eat food family-style, get big hugs like family, and pay prices that you would only charge your family. No strangers, no reminders of work. The restaurant had become a brand—for me and for many others. I would go way out of my way for it, regardless of its location.

I know this example is a restaurant, and you might think that it's vastly different from a more traditional brand advertised on television, such as a brand of deodorant. While there certainly are many differences, a restaurant is as much a brand as any other product or service. The principles of good brand management hold true whether the brand is a restaurant, a laundry detergent, a small retail boutique, a box of cookies, or anything else. The experience effect should still be present.

The principles of good brand management hold true whether the brand is a restaurant, a laundry detergent, a small retail boutique, a box of cookies, or anything else.

I offer this personal experience at my favorite restaurant as a way to illustrate the importance of the experience effect. Creating and sticking to something that works for the brand and for consumers is the key to loyalty and success over the long haul. Not that the brand can't grow, change, and evolve. It absolutely can and in fact must evolve over time. Growing and evolving is part of the experience, certainly. But it must be done consciously, consistently, and in sync with consumers and how they are changing and growing.

When done right, the experience effect defines the brand, at least in the minds of consumers, even as it evolves over time. It positions the brand in their minds and beautifully keeps it there through every interaction. This is why it is so vitally important.

I often hear marketers debating about positioning, and it always makes me smile. Positioning should be easy to define. The problem is that marketers often confuse positioning with claims or with the product category where the brand competes. Positioning is not a product claim or product attribute. It's not the ability to fill in wrinkles around the eye nor is it the range of vitamins in a breakfast cereal. Suffice it to say that positioning is the place that the brand holds in the minds of consumers. It's a lot more than just the product claim or the category, because that would be too generic and too rational, and everyone in a category would have the same positioning. Essentially, positioning is how we want the consumer to think about our brand. It should differentiate; product attributes don't tend to do that since most brands in a category offer very similar claims and attributes. Take a look at the skin care category and you'll see what I mean. Any given set of skin care brands can make the same kinds of claims to eliminate wrinkles. The differentiation comes in how the brands are positioned, whether they are wholesome like Neutrogena, professional like Olay, or scientific like L'Oréal. Consumers have the opportunity to choose among these brands and how they are positioned. Positioning should be unique to the brand and to the consumers who embrace it. It is the mix of rational and emotional experiences, much like I described with my favorite restaurant in New York and much like with J.Crew, as I noted in the Prologue.

The brand experiences actually become the positioning in consumers' minds, and the experience effect is what puts it there. That's why it's so important to understand it, to get it right, and to keep it consistent. It ultimately determines how consumers feel about the brand and how they attach meaning and value to the brand. It's also what will differentiate the brand from other brands in the same category.

My experiences at my favorite restaurant firmly put an impression in my mind of what that brand was all about. I knew why I would go to that restaurant, who I would bring with me, how much money I should have in my pocket, and what I expected to get out of the evening. The funny thing is that this restaurant never accepted credit cards nor did it sell alcohol, which was also consistent with the brand experience. The bills were never that big so I always had enough cash on hand. My experiences at my favorite restaurant shaped how I compared that restaurant with others I might be considering, shaped my choices in how I wanted to spend my money, and positioned the restaurant firmly in my mind.

It was always clear to me what I was going to get from that restaurant versus a place like La Grenouille in midtown New York, which is the epitome of fine French dining and a very different restaurant experience. La Grenouille is over-the-top culinary luxury, where food enthusiasts are enveloped by exquisite service and the most beautiful floral arrangements that I have ever seen. Walking into that restaurant is like walking into a fragrant culinary escape, complete with perfectly prepared dishes that delight all the senses. I go to La Grenouille on very special occasions as much for the food as for the service as for the flowers—completely different from Sunday nights at my favorite little neighborhood Italian restaurant. The portions are tiny but incredibly rich. The service is much more formal and professional. No hugs and kisses and certainly no heaping bowls of spaghetti with meatballs. I have these two restaurants perfectly positioned in my mind as two completely different experiences, and I choose one over the other depending on my certain needs for a dining experience.

The experience effect is so important to marketers because it:

- Defines the brand for consumers

- Positions the brand in consumers' minds

- Differentiates the brand from competitors

- Helps consumers make good choices and appropriate purchase decisions

- Builds brand loyalty

- Justifies a price point, whether high or low

- Brings calm and stability to an otherwise chaotic life

So we better concentrate on building it right! Let's look at a few real brand examples to bring the point home.

Tylenol is a classic example of how the experience effect helps define the brand, give it meaning, and differentiate it from its competition. Tylenol is perceived as being safe, caring, and nurturing. This is best exemplified in its handling of the famous Tylenol crisis back in the early 1980s, when the company reacted quickly and selflessly to several incidents of product tampering where consumers died from poisons put into the product. The company immediately took responsibility and pulled the products off shelves across the country without missing a beat. The move cost the company hundreds of millions of dollars, yet it cemented its positioning in consumers' minds as a trusted, responsible company. The brand also took the initiative to install tamper-proof mechanisms on all of its packaging despite the increased cost of production, thus bearing the burden of making sure its consumers were safe.

So no wonder it makes sense that the Tylenol brand would have a full line of nurturing products suitable for all ages for alleviating pain, reducing fever, and relieving the common cold. Of course, the brand's marketing campaigns have done a great job of reinforcing the brand's nurturing positioning as well. Even the current campaign is focused on giving lifestyle tips on staying well in addition to specific product claims of efficacy.

Tylenol has created and owned years and years of a consistent brand experience, perhaps not always perfect, perhaps not always successful in the marketplace, but always unique and meaningful for sure.

Marriott is yet another well-defined example of how the experience effect also helps consumers make appropriate choices. I know that whenever I travel on business, I try to stay at a Marriott hotel, and not just for the loyalty points, although the Marriott Rewards program is a key part of the brand experience. In my mind, Marriott is convenient, professional lodging for the busy business traveler. I generally know what kind of accommodations I'm going to get at a Marriott hotel, regardless of the city. Calling the toll-free number or logging onto the website makes for an easy reservation process. And of course the Marriott Rewards program provides a nice incentive to stay loyal to the brand on future trips.

I don't stay at a Marriott hotel when I'm traveling with my family. I don't find it relaxing to be surrounded by business travelers and to be constantly reminded of work. For pleasure travel, I make other choices. I've positioned Marriott as my work option, my hotel of choice for when I make business trips. Now I know that Marriott also has exclusive resorts in exotic destinations, but truthfully, that doesn't work for me as a consumer. I've positioned the hotel as a business hotel and that's when I choose to engage in the brand. Of course, a business seminar at an exotic destination isn't a bad choice for business travel. The Marriott experience has helped me make choices that work for my life, for my business needs specifically. And the Marriott website certainly makes it easy for me to book my travel, for any need or destination. There is easy navigation dedicated to business travel and there is even an option called "QuickGroup" for booking group meetings and conferences. It's also easy to find hotel availability by searching hotel location, metro area, or date. For mobile users, there's even an iPhone app. It couldn't be easier for loyal Marriott business travelers, making it that much more of a logical choice for arranging business travel needs.

Nike is also a comprehensive example of how the experience effect can build brand loyalty. Nike offers high-performance sportswear for athletes of all levels. Everything Nike does reinforces my positive perceptions of the brand and of its positioning. I relate to it. I know I'm not a professional athlete, never have been and never will be. But I work out really hard almost every day, so I relate to what Nike tells me and to what it offers me, and I am intensely loyal to the brand as a result. I have the sneakers, shorts, and sweats, all of it. The way Nike has built its brand experience—including advertising, website, flagship stores, retail displays, endorsements from professional athletes, and of course products—has consistently built my loyalty over time. I know exactly what I am going to get from Nike. There are no surprises, only high-performance sportswear like what the pros use.

Mercedes-Benz is a high-end example of how the experience effect can actually justify a price point. Mercedes-Benz is the ultimate luxury for the discriminating driver. For those who love the brand, they are the most beautiful, luxurious cars in the world. The entire car-buying experience with Mercedes-Benz has been documented and studied as best in class, from the showrooms themselves to the test drive. The collateral material is beautiful and the salespeople are obviously proud to hand it out, with gorgeous car shots that make it seem like the photographer is as much in love with the car as anyone.

After the purchase, the service and parts department has been known for consistent, high-performance, white-glove customer service that is second to none. The department even picks up the car and provides a loaner for any kind of service needed, including regularly scheduled checkups. Service comes complete with roadside assistance and a "Happy Birthday" letter every single year. Other brands may have similar programs, but when all of these things add up, for those who own and love a Mercedes-Benz, the experience justifies the price.

These are all great examples, and if we were to stretch our minds and think about it even further, the experience effect is so important that it can ultimately bring calm and stability to an otherwise oversaturated life. Marketing done well means that as a consumer you know what you are going to get. No surprises, no disappointments, no buyer's regret. If you try something once and don't like it, you don't have to try it again until the brand gives you a new reason. If you fall in love with a brand, you can love it over and over again and not have to question or worry.

The experience effect is so important that it can ultimately bring calm and stability to an otherwise oversaturated life.

The experience effect done well means that consumers can expand their interactions with the brand and have an understanding of what it will deliver. Consumers can experiment with line extensions or visit a website after shopping a retail location without being disappointed. It might not be the exact same experience, and probably shouldn't be, but it will certainly be consistent. This is one of the emotional benefits behind brand loyalty, and it's a direct result of the experience effect. How else can we explain using only Tide liquid to do laundry, or going out of the way to find a Diet Coke even when there's a Diet Pepsi right there? How else do you explain the joy of just grabbing a favorite Reach toothbrush off the drugstore shelf and not having to sort through hundreds of options, including the store brands, every shopping trip? The experience effect helps consumers make quick, intelligent choices based on their history with the brand and saves them brain space for more challenging things that come up in their day.

CHAPTER 3

Brand Soundtrack

Making the Right Decisions for the Brand

LET'S GET INTO IT! How on earth should we get started? With so many ways to begin our journey, it can easily get overwhelming. Fortunately there's a simple first step that will put us on the right path to developing a successful experience effect.

I've always held the conviction that starting with the consumer is the only way to go. Consumers will guide every step of our development, from beginning to end. But before we start analyzing consumers, their behaviors, and their attitudes, there is something we absolutely must do first. We first need to make a few decisions to define our brand, including basic stuff like what category we compete in, what claims we can deliver, and what promises we want to make. Then we can turn to more intricate things like brand style, character, and personality. It's not that we are not thinking about consumers at this point, it's just that we have to lay a little groundwork for the brand before we can concentrate on our consumers.

Certainly, defining the brand goes hand in hand with understanding consumers, so we can't do one without the other. Good marketing always starts and ends with the consumer, but it's hard to do that without some fundamental decisions about the brand at the outset. Since we'll be devoting so much of the book to consumers, it's best to start the process with defining the brand. We need to know our brand before we can really start doing any of the work for the experience effect.

When defining a brand like Olay, for example, the brand managers know that it is in the skin care and beauty business. The brand managers also know the kind of claims that each product in the lineup can make, and they have a general understanding of the promises that the brand and its products offer. Olay first knows what Olay is all about, and then the marketers determine how the brand can deliver it to consumers. From this basic starting point, they can begin to focus on the more in-depth consumer needs and wants.

We need to define the brand in a few key areas:

- What business is the brand in?

- What does the brand deliver to consumers and what promises can it make? Specifically, are there any supportable claims?

- What does the brand stand for?

- To some extent, what is the brand's personality, style, or character?

- To some extent, what is the brand's voice?

This is by no means an official or exhaustive list. It's just an attempt to outline some of the basics of the brand before building the experience effect for it. Let's take a look at the M&M's brand and answer some basic brand definition questions.

The brand definition of M&M's clearly sets the stage for how the brand managers will market the brand and how they will build multiple brand experiences across the landscape of the various products, websites, advertising campaigns, promotions, and retail locations:

- M&M's is in the candy business, from a rational perspective. From an emotional perspective we could also say that the brand is in the escapism business.

- M&M's delivers bite-size chocolates in multiple colors, from a rational perspective. We could also say from an emotional perspective that it delivers a personal moment of indulgence.

- M&M's promises a little pop of good fun. It is also innocent and frivolous.

These are my words, meant to illustrate the point that this kind of clear definition for M&M's sets the specific path for developing the marketing.

Check out the brand's marketing. Every aspect of the M&M's experience is cool and engaging, and a little pop of fun. The television advertising is incredibly colorful, lighthearted, carefree, and spontaneous, whether featuring one of the M&M's characters at a

Have you ever ordered personalized M&M's in your favorite colors or limited edition flavors? Or holiday M&M's with cheerful messages on them? It's quite an experience, completely consistent with the M&M's brand definition.

red carpet event or just highlighting tens of thousands of colorful M&M's rolling around in an ever-changing landscape. The website is equally colorful and engaging, although much deeper and richer in content than the advertising; yet it is entirely consistent with the brand definition. The website features custom ordering, recipes, and games that the advertising cannot possibly offer in thirty seconds, all with the same brand personality and character.

Have you ever ordered personalized M&M's in your favorite colors or limited edition flavors like white and milk chocolate in a raspberry or orange shell, only available from the MyMMs.com website? Or holiday M&M's with cheerful messages on them? It's quite an experience, completely consistent with the M&M's brand definition. It costs so little to have so much colorful fun.

To get the full M&M's experience, visit M&M's World in Times Square, New York, or in Las Vegas. It's an exact dramatization of the M&M's brand with all of its splendor and movement, only this time live and in person. The characters greet visitors right at the door and sometimes even come outside for photo opportunities. Huge billboards show rolling landscapes of colorful M&M's, much like the advertising, but now even larger than life in 3-D color. The characters also roam the floors, happily stopping to say hello to the kids and to help pick out a funky M&M's toy uniquely merchandised on the shelf. You won't ever want to leave this candy world because you feel like you've escaped the real world for a few minutes. And that's exactly what a bag of M&M's is like—a quick little escape from the world. All for around a buck! The brand managers of M&M's through the years have made conscious decisions about how they want to define their brand, with a lot of input and learning from consumers of course. And they continuously build the brand experience across multiple elements to deliver on it.

Sure, they have stumbled a few times through the years, but it has not hurt them terribly. Take for instance M&M's Premiums, made from luxury chocolate packaged in high-prestige cardboard boxes at an indulgent price point. It doesn't make a lot of sense if you know and love the M&M's brand. M&M's exquisitely luxurious? I don't think so. More like pure innocent fun. I believe that M&M's Premiums is inconsistent with the core M&M's brand. It is a calculated risk that could end up being a marketing mistake— most brands make a mistake or two as they continually try to evolve and grow. It is best to experiment and take chances while developing your brand's experience effect. Without experimentation, there is no marketing innovation.

Compare this to Hershey's Kisses, a direct competitor of M&M's because it arguably is also an amusing brand. Hershey's also has a similar product entry in the premium chocolate category, Hershey's Bliss. Notice that the brand managers don't call that brand Hershey's Kisses Premium. The premium chocolate option is marketed under Hershey's Bliss, with a different brand definition and a different brand name. I consider this to be smart portfolio management of brands and brand definitions in order to offer consumers multiple choices without causing brand confusion.

> *Many brands deliver a strong point of view, and it becomes a key ingredient to their brand definition.*

Another way to define the brand is to understand what it stands for. This might not work for every brand, but it can be a cornerstone for some. Many brands deliver a strong point of view, and it becomes a key ingredient to their brand definition.

Like Durex condoms. The brand stands for sexual well-being. On the website, loud and clear, it says, "Sex plays a fundamental role in our physical and emotional well-being. We believe that a healthy and rewarding sex life should be for everyone to enjoy." The brand managers have clearly decided that sexual well-being is the brand platform or brand definition. The brand has a strong point of view around sexual well-being, and everything it does delivers on it, from the educational information that the brand distributes to the charitable causes it supports, even to the gaming found on the website.

This definition clearly influences new product introductions, which have to stand behind sexual well-being as part of the brand definition. Of course you may wonder why Durex lags so far behind the dominant market leader, Trojan, which arguably also has a distinctive experience effect. I believe that Trojan's brand leadership is based more on consistent and aggressive marketing spending. In the United States, Trojan outspends Durex many times over. That doesn't mean that the Durex brand hasn't made good decisions about its brand definition. In other parts of the world, Durex is the number one brand—the marketing economics in the U.S. market are just a little different.

Marketers can also define a brand by its natural abilities or the abilities that have been purposefully built for the brand. Don't define the brand or take a stand on something that the product can't deliver. Don't promise something that isn't possible for the brand. But if the brand has a built-in ability to do something unique and meaningful, then use it as part of the brand definition. A lot of food brands are defined this way, for the nutritional value that they bring.

Don't promise sexual well-being and build your brand all around it if you can't live up to it. Every part of the brand experience should live up to that definition. For Durex, every part of the brand is built around sexual well-being, including every product in the brand's lineup and every interaction with consumers. If it holds true to its definition, consumers should never see any new product or new marketing communication that is inconsistent with sexual well-being.

The challenge here is to create a brand definition that is unique to the category. Don't build a brand definition around something that the entire category can also promise. And make sure that the brand can actually deliver on the definition. Don't promise a food product loaded with vitamins and minerals if the product can't deliver on consumer expectations of nutritional content. Diet Coke Plus (with vitamins) suffered quite a bit because the product did not deliver the kind of nutritional value expected from a beverage claiming health benefits. Simply adding a few token vitamins to a beverage otherwise perceived as "unhealthy" did not live up to consumer expectations.

Wal-Mart is another great example. Wal-Mart defines the brand around offering everyday low prices and saving consumers money. "Save Money. Live Better" is the Wal-Mart brand promise. Wal-Mart certainly has built the ability to deliver it. The company walks the walk in every way. If you have ever been a service or marketing partner to Wal-Mart, then you know exactly what I mean. Wal-Mart has created not only an entire brand experience around everyday low prices, but also an infrastructure to deliver it, such as having distribution channels and supplier relationships specifically organized to keep costs low.

Of course, Wal-Mart is infamous for its strict policies, and it has received considerable criticism for unfair supplier policies and for unfair competition against local mom-and-pop retailers. Even in New York City, Wal-Mart has had considerable difficulties breaking into the marketplace because of the company's anti-union policies, which are counter to the business culture in New York but a key ingredient in Wal-Mart's infrastructure. Founder Sam Walton built the company from the ground up to deliver on the brand definition of everyday low prices. He ended up changing the face of retail marketing and big business as a result.

Kmart, historically one of Wal-Mart's biggest competitors, can't seem to keep up with Wal-Mart, maybe because it can't keep up with the Wal-Mart experience effect. For me personally, I can very clearly define the Wal-Mart brand, but I cannot so easily define the Kmart brand. This is true for each brand experience as well. Unlike Wal-Mart, Kmart is incredibly inconsistent from store to store, and the retail locations in no way live up to the imagery as presented in the advertising. For the most part, I can't explain what Kmart promises its consumers. Martha Stewart together with a "blue light special" is a little hard to reconcile as a consumer.

Personality and style also have a lot to do with defining the brand and building the experience effect. Should the brand be fun and carefree like M&M's? Then the brand experience should reflect that—like M&M's does with colors and a great sense of humor. Should the brand be serious and professional? Then the brand experience needs to reflect that—like Oral-B toothbrushes, for example.

Marketers call this brand personality, brand character, or brand style, which are all the same thing, really, although many try to draw subtle distinctions. Think about the personality and style that the brand should have before starting to build the experience effect. It is true that we need some understanding of the consumer here, but defining the brand's personality will still make the building process a lot smoother at every step. It sometimes helps to ascribe a celebrity face to the brand to help define it. It's an enlightening exercise that you should try with your team-mates. Is the brand personality more like Justin Timberlake, Meryl Streep, Jennifer Aniston, or Jack Black? More like Marge Simpson or Will Smith?

> *Is the brand personality more like Justin Timberlake, Meryl Streep, Jennifer Aniston, or Jack Black?*

Attaching a well-known celebrity to the brand can help bring a visual and real element to the brand definition. No consumer in the world will ever see this, but almost everyone on the brand team can relate and participate. Put a celebrity face to the other brands in the category as well, and you will get a clear definition of how the brands differ. Line them all up along a wall to get a broad sense of the varying brand personalities within the category.

If the wall is full of pictures of Paris Hilton, then there's obviously an opportunity to differentiate the brand in the category. We often do this when launching new brands as a quick visual test to see where the brand can fit into the category from a style, personality, and brand definition perspective.

The M&M's brand is most like, well, the M&M's brand characters. They've become celebrities in their own right. Hershey's Kisses might be more like Eva Longoria, whereas Godiva chocolate might be more like a celebrity chef such as Giada De Laurentiis. It's an interesting way to look at it, right?

Another creative exercise in defining the brand is to put together a brand soundtrack, almost like for a movie. Put together a collection of music that best captures the desired brand personality and definition. You will need to make a lot of tough decisions when selecting these songs—trust me! Compile a range of songs that reflects the various aspects of the brand and that is also in line with the brand's consumers. Try to put together sound-tracks for the competition as well. The soundtrack can become not only a way to illustrate the brand definition, but also a great present for all the team members and a way to rally them togeth-er, while at the same time bringing creativity to the work.

As we define the brand, we also need to think through how the competition defines their brands, with or without the celebrity faces or soundtracks as tools, particularly if the category is highly competitive. We will want to know how our brand definition com-pares to the others in the category. We'll want to define the brand in the context of the category and the other brands within it. Strategic planners will often construct a perceptual map of a cat-egory and literally plot the brands on the map in context with one another. It is a visual way to illustrate the brand definition.

A perceptual map is just one way to define the brands in con-text with one another, but I have found it to be a very simple and useful tool, something that can be done in a quick snapshot. The goal is to have the brand in a spot of its own on that perceptual map, where no other brand lives. Otherwise consumers will either be confused or they will switch back and forth between brands, putting more pressure on building loyalty and on constantly win-ning them back. The perceptual map is a great tool to help carve out a unique spot in the category. It helps reduce a complicated situation to a simple, action-oriented visual to help guide deci-sions, much like the visuals of celebrities mentioned already, but in a more serious way.

There are many kinds of perceptual maps. They can be multi-dimensional and they can certainly take great effort to build. Start simple. You should consider the perceptual map to be a simple four-quadrant diagram that is formed by the intersection of two axes, one horizontal and one vertical. Let's have the horizontal axis (the x-axis) represent one dimension of the category and the vertical axis (the y-axis) represent another dimension of the category. As we identify these dimensions, we will pick two different elements that truly define the category and that ultimately can define how the brand fits within the category in context with the other brands. Each axis represents that dimension in a range or a spectrum. Call it from light to dark, from low to high, or from off to on, depending on the dimension.

For example, in fashion one of the dimensions might be style. For cookies one dimension might be sweetness. For cars one dimension might be performance. Of course in any category, one dimension can always be cost, if cost is a relative benchmark. These examples are obviously not very specific, so the more specific we can make the dimensions for the category, then the more definitive the perceptual map will be. The placement of the brands on the map will also be more descriptive.

There are many ways to build the perceptual map, but try to pick two different dimensions that describe the category. Ideally, pick one that is rational and one that is emotional. We will talk a lot more about the importance of the emotional dimension in chapter six. Stay consistent and put the rational dimension on the x-axis and the emotional one on the y-axis. Just make sure that both dimensions are relevant and important to the category, specifically to the consumers in the category. See figure 3.1 on the next page for a template of a perceptual map.

For fashion jewelry, the dimensions could be price on the x-axis (rational) and style or social status on the y-axis (emotional). Or for cars, foul-weather performance could be on the x-axis and social status on the y-axis. Each axis should portray the spectrum, so it might convey low price to high price on the x-axis and classic style to trendy style on the y-axis, to continue with the fashion jewelry example. The truth is that for any given category, we could come up with several dimensions, both rational and emotional. When this is true, then pick the two that are the most defining for the category, or build more than one perceptual map to help define

---

FIGURE 3.1   Perceptual Map

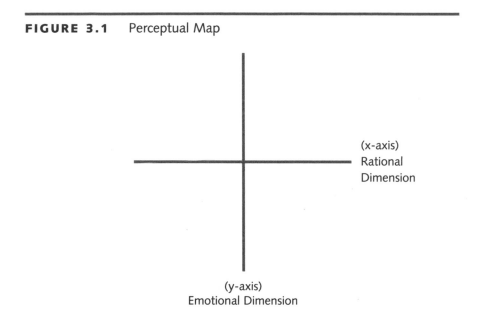

(x-axis)
Rational
Dimension

(y-axis)
Emotional Dimension

the brand even more completely. With two or three perceptual maps in hand for the brand, you will have a clear-cut brand definition to start building the experience effect. Feel free to get creative and build multidimensional perceptual maps. Multidimensional perceptual maps get very crazy very quickly, however, and you might end up losing the clarity of the point.

Either way, do what's best to help make decisions around the brand definition. Remember that the point of the exercise is to define the brand so that it has a unique spot in the category. If we were to use the M&M's example again, a perceptual map of the candy category may look like the one in figure 3.2.

Note that the map has the two axes as we've been discussing, each with a defining attribute that portrays the category along a spectrum. In this case, the horizontal x-axis is inexpensive versus expensive (rational) and the vertical y-axis is serious versus fun (emotional).

FIGURE 3.2   M&M's Perceptual Map (with Dimensions)

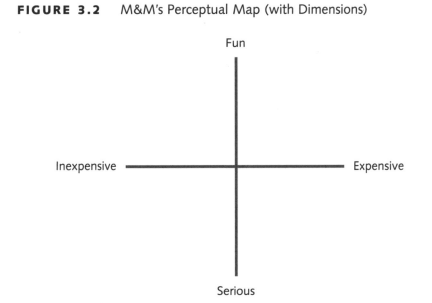

When you plot the brands onto the perceptual map, you'll see that M&M's is in a very different place from Godiva, Toblerone, or Ghirardelli. But it's relatively close to Hershey's Kisses. This is a great way to show how the brand definition sits relative to the competition (see figure 3.3).

Now stick M&M's Premiums and Hershey's Bliss onto the perceptual map (see figure 3.4).

Pretty enlightening, right? Perceptual maps really help marketers to visualize a complex category simply and to see how the brands are defined within it. Now see what happens with two different, more definitive dimensions that are more unusual than using cheap versus expensive and serious versus fun. How about candy-coated versus pure chocolate and independently indulgent versus meant for sharing, as shown in figure 3.5. Wow, what a difference!

FIGURE 3.3   M&M's Perceptual Map (with Brands Plotted)

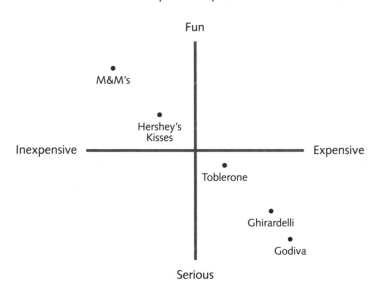

FIGURE 3.4   M&M's Perceptual Map (with More Brands Plotted)

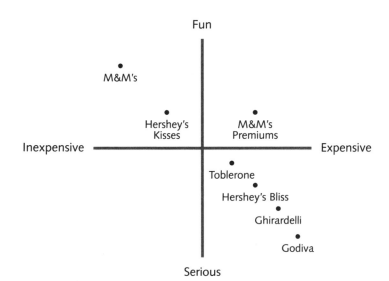

FIGURE 3.5   M&M's Perceptual Map (with New Dimensions)

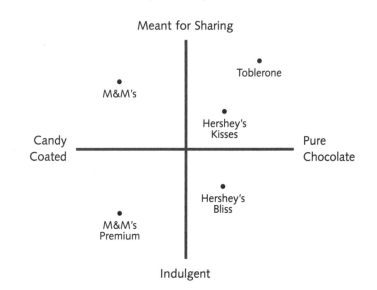

Keep in mind that these dimensions and placements are all debatable; you may perceive these brands very differently, and certainly the brand managers may have a different take. The point here is that with more specific dimensions, an even clearer definition of the brand pops out. I'd recommend using two or three perceptual maps to help visualize the brand definition. Get into it. This is actually a great team exercise that ends up being very interesting because different team members will often create different perceptual maps, even when using the same dimensions. Lots of debate will lead to great decisions about the brand.

The same team may have very different perceptions of the brand definition. Before creating the experience effect, make sure you have agreement across the entire team! We will talk more in chapter fifteen about how to get alignment across the team.

Before creating the experience effect, make sure you have agreement across the entire team!

Remember that you can create a perceptual map using all sorts of attributes. The attributes can be product features, consumer benefits, and emotional feelings. You should decide what is important as differentiators in the category.

Just to make the point, I purposefully chose two very simple attributes, but you should explore going much deeper to help define the brand, like I did with the second set of dimensions. Go even deeper to get an even better definition. Notice that in my simple example I chose a rational attribute and an emotional one. Purposefully and consistently, always use rational and emotional components. When we dive deeper into consumer understanding in the next few chapters you'll see why having both dimensions brings a much deeper meaning to the brand. Marketers create perceptual maps using a careful selection of the attributes that are the most important to their consumers on emotional and rational dimensions. Up-front consumer research helps guide them on what the most important attributes are to their consumers, which we will explore in later chapters as well.

Great marketers always make sure their brand is defined by a distinct space on a perceptual map, or they go back and redefine the brand. This or any kind of perceptual mapping should be done way before we even begin to develop the experience effect. Finding a distinct space in the category helps to make sure that the brand experience is strategically unique and completely ownable. Of course there are many ways to help make the brand experience ownable, some more strategically based and others more executional. It's important to think through these techniques as you define your brand. We'll discuss ways to make the experience effect ownable in chapter thirteen.

We began this chapter by asking ourselves how to get started. Before we can start to build the experience effect, we must first define what the brand is all about and what it stands for. We need to make sure the brand can fulfill its definition, and we need to build into the brand definition a personality and style that's truly unique. We need to determine where the competition lies as well, so that the brand definition can occupy a distinct space in the category. Just keep the consumer in mind the entire time.

CHAPTER 4

Not by Numbers Alone

Understanding the Brand's Target Audience

I TELL ALL MY TEAMMATES and clients to always start every marketing discussion and every program development with the consumer. Good marketing starts and ends with the consumer, and never stops in between. As marketers, we should be thinking about our consumers with everything we do, even when we are defining the brand, as we did in the previous chapter.

Serving the wants and needs of our consumers should be our sole motivation during every step of developing the experience effect. As marketers, it's important for us to have the voice of the consumer in all of our marketing decisions. We need to ask ourselves key consumer questions at every step, such as:

- Will the toothbrush packaging innovation be easy for consumers to use, and will they understand how to open it? Will the packaging have shelf impact at retail so that consumers can find it at their favorite store?

- Will the facial cleanser fragrance make consumers feel clean and refreshed like the brand claims? Will the fragrance entice consumers to buy the brand repeatedly?

- Does the laundry detergent sales forecast reflect current trends in consumer consumption behavior? Is it realistic to assume that the consumer will repeat the purchase cycle that we are planning?

Let the consumer answer all the key questions in the marketing plan. Get to know consumers and continually strive to understand them, so that we can give them exactly what they want and need. The consumer I am referring to here is the target market identified for the brand.

Before we can start to understand consumers, we obviously need to identify who they are—we need to define the target market, much like we defined the brand. Of course, defining the target market goes hand-in-hand with understanding it. We can't define something that we don't understand! We need to do both, often at the same time, particularly if the brand is new to the market. It's much like the work we did to define the brand in chapter three.

So from a targeting perspective, decide if the consumer target market:

- Makes sense for the brand from a business standpoint

- Best fits the brand and its offerings

- Is most likely to relate to the brand definition

- Has unmet needs in the category that the brand can fill

Define the target up front, and then start to understand it.

One of the hardest parts about marketing is making smart choices. We all need to make smart business decisions if we want to generate positive results. One of those hard choices is picking the target consumer. Choosing whom to target is one of the brand's biggest marketing decisions.

There may be more than one target if the business and the resources are big enough, but many times we are forced to choose one core audience. Since women tend to be the purchasers in the household, more often than not the target is a woman at a specific stage of her life. When the brand definition is big enough and when the brand truly understands its consumers, one target audience is often more than enough to sustain the business.

It's important to recognize that no one brand can be all things to all people. One brand can't possibly satisfy both men and women, young and old, liberal and conservative. Nor could

> *No one brand can be all things to all people.*

one brand satisfy the needs of the urban and rural, wealthy and poor, trendy and classic, all with the same brand definition and the same set of offerings. By trying to be everything, the brand will end up being nothing at all. And every step of the marketing process will be more difficult because a critical move was not made up front: deciding on the target market and focusing on its specific needs.

Sure, the politicians try to do this—and they are classic examples of trying to satisfy all people. Think about it:

- How many politicians are successful in pleasing the majority of people?

- How many politicians actually get much done?

- How many politicians have a good brand identity?

The same could be asked about brands that try to please too many target markets. Ironically, we could be asking those same questions about brands, politicians, or many of the people in our lives. That's a topic for chapter eleven!

If there is more than one target market, make sure that the targets are not at odds with each other. It would be difficult, for example, to create a fragrance for both men and for women, although Calvin Klein did it with ck one as a rare exception. Or even a fragrance for both teenage girls and for adult women of different ages. The targets have distinctly different needs and desires, hence the brands may have distinctly different definitions.

Try to understand which target is a better opportunity for the brand, and run with it. It's virtually impossible to define the target audience without understanding it, and it's virtually impossible to define the brand without understanding the target audience; the two processes go hand-in-hand. Of course this all depends on the level of tenure that the brand has in the marketplace. Some of these issues may already be resolved. It's then our job as marketers to continually evolve the brand and to focus on the most productive areas. It's our job to make sure that the decisions are still appropriate in the changing marketplace and with changing consumer wants and needs.

In some ways, I see the Gap retail store as trying too hard to be all things to all people. On the one hand it is trendy and stylish, but on the other it is basic and rugged. It is both down-home and celebrity at the same time. It is for anyone and everyone: women and men, babies, kids, and young adults. The brand hit its stride in the mid-1990s mostly because it identified a core target audience who embraced the product line and what it stood for at the time: easy, relaxed clothing at affordable prices for young, casually stylish adults. It was the first big denim brand to take over the space that Levi's left a bit vacant, much like Starbucks did with its coffee shops. That core Gap audience has grown up, however, and presumably their needs have evolved. The Gap brand has lost touch with its core audience and has not replaced it with a well-defined alternative.

I see the Gap brand as trying to fulfill too many people's needs, and as a result I'm not sure it's satisfying very many at all. In the brand's advertising in the past few years, it has attempted to use high-style celebrities in "weekend" wear, it has attempted the "hot model" approach and the "everybody" approach. The brand is still behind the charity route with (RED).

> The Gap brand has lost touch with its core audience and has not replaced it with a well-defined alternative.

The brand offers clothes for babies, kids, and adults, and also underwear, exercise clothes, maternity items, and outerwear, all featured in different ways in the advertising and in multiple stores, resulting in what I believe is a lack of true identity. The website is downright confusing because there are so many options to navigate to get to the various brand offerings (women, men, maternity, kids, and babies), but also too many ways to navigate to the other brands in the company portfolio (Old Navy, Banana Republic, Athleta, and Piperlime). Plus there are promotional offers and featured products to choose (free shipping, save 20 percent at Old Navy, and save 10 percent on Tuesdays), none of which are presented in any kind of communications priority. This is a clear sign that the brand has not refined its targeting or its brand definition.

Do a Google search for "gap" and the first item that appears says, "Here you'll find the best picks in men's clothing, women's clothing, plus maternity, kids, and baby clothing as well." The next item on that same search says, "Gap Kids clothing is known for style, durability, and value: activewear, school uniforms, graphic Ts, hooded sweatshirts, polos, pants, jeans, and more." Notice the laundry list. Trying to do too much? I suspect so.

Carefully define the brand and then choose the target market specifically, knowing that the brand can uniquely fill the needs of those consumers. And then get to know the consumer better than the competition does. You'll be well on your way to building the brand's experience effect.

Compare Gap to its competition, like Abercrombie & Fitch, and witness another brand that perhaps has a clearer definition of their target market and a deeper understanding of their consumers. As a parallel exercise, do a Google search for "abercrombie & fitch"; the first item that appears says, "The highest quality, casual, All-American lifestyle clothing for aspirational men and women," meaning college-age, good looking, incredibly fit, and popular, just like we all want to be! The next item on that same search specifies men and says, "Rugged, high quality clothing designed for the casual college lifestyle." Still a lot of words, but a much more well-defined brand that appears to understand its target market better. Interestingly, Abercrombie & Fitch has more than one target market, young men and young women, yet both have the same aspiration. It certainly seems that the brand understands both of its consumer segments quite well and that there are enough commonalities between them to avoid a branding conflict. The commonalities lie around a "certain sort" of young man and young woman who would be attracted to the casual college lifestyle that Abercrombie & Fitch promotes. But if you notice, the stores have distinct spaces for men and women so that the brand can still satisfy each target market's specific clothing needs at the point of purchase.

Abercrombie & Fitch even has a successful kids' brand called abercrombie. Notice the single word and lowercase in the branding. Smart. Distinct offerings for the distinct target markets. Each brand is focused on the specific target market with a specific understanding of it, rather than just trying to appeal to all people like Gap. Abercrombie & Fitch stays focused on the aspirational youth market, so it's only natural that the company would also have a starter brand like abercrombie to build its own future consumers (targeted to their moms).

You could say the same about Gap with its line of clothing for babies and kids, but the brand is still not as clearly defined as Abercrombie & Fitch's. It tries to be all things to all people, all at the same time, rather than picking one type of consumer and fulfilling those specific needs.

I have to commend the consistent and focused targeting in sync with the brand definition of Abercrombie & Fitch. Most targeting combines a bit of demographics with a bit of psychographics—this is certainly the case with Abercrombie & Fitch, where it's less about the age and more about the attitude. To really understand the target consumers, we need to learn about them on many dimensions. If we really want to know how to build an experience effect, we need to understand both the demographics and psychographics of the target group.

The demographics of the target market are just one dimension of understanding. Perhaps the first, but still only one dimension. Demographics form the base of knowledge about our consumers and can include information such as:

- Age and sex

- Household income and education level

- Geographic location and language spoken

- Marital status and parenthood, including ages of the children in the household

These demographic facts, and many others, form the statistical and factual base of the target market. They can provide a surface understanding of the size of the target market and some basic statistics about the population within it. Remember that demographics are reported as numbers, and averages of numbers at that. Averages can hide a lot of meaning, so we'll need to fill in the consumer picture with a lot more detail and texture. Demographics can't answer how a consumer feels about the brand or about the category. Demographics might answer "who" and "where" and "what," but the numbers generally can't answer "how" and "why."

> Gone are the days where we can simply study the demographics of a target market and feel like we've truly gotten to know it.

Gone are the days where we can simply study the demographics of a target market and feel like we've truly gotten to know it. There are many other factors we need to understand if we are going to build a tailored brand experience for our consumers. For example, not all consumers of the same age think, feel, and behave the same way. It is true that members of the baby boomer generation have been known to exhibit similar tendencies, for example in their work ethic. But we need to be careful not to overgeneralize and thereby hide the insights that might help us truly understand consumers. There are certainly many pockets of baby boomers that behave differently from the norm for their age group. In any age group this is true with any demographic measure. It is often said that the younger generations have a sense of entitlement and don't want to work too hard. I've met many a young talent who is an exception to that generalization.

There are also people of other age groups who exhibit the same behavior as their older baby boomer counterparts, even though they are much younger. Also, not all people in the same income level exhibit the same purchasing behavior in a given category. Because of this, we need to add in some other factors and dimensions to really understand the target market, regardless of what the demographics might tell us.

We also need to look at the psychographics of consumers— their attitudes, interests, emotions, opinions, and behaviors. It's how consumers feel about a brand, category, or topic of interest, and how they behave. For example, how do people in a target market feel about imported goods? Feelings about products made outside of the United States is a good example of a psychographic, and it can greatly determine the success of certain brands and product categories.

We can start to segment consumers based on their psychographics as well as their demographics. Psychographics are a propensity to feel, think, and act a certain way, and they often have little to do with a demographic statistic like age or income. This serves to add more dimension to the targeting.

Perhaps the biggest aspect of psychographics is behavior. It's a study of what people do in certain situations. Commuting behavior on the way to work is one example. We can learn a lot about the differences between people who spend fifteen minutes commuting back and forth to work versus those who spend an hour and a half. For example, we can learn a lot about their media consumption behavior, which is likely to have nothing to do with many of their demographics.

How you might reach consumers based on commuting behavior can vastly differ. For example, those commuting via public transportation may be more likely to read a newspaper online, listen to a podcast, or use a mobile device. Subway riders may be more likely to actually read outdoor advertising than those who are driving in a car.

Shopping behavior is another psychographic that can shed a tremendous amount of light on a consumer target, particularly women. I spent years creating retail promotions for clients, across many categories of consumer packaged goods, like over-the-counter drugs, health and beauty aids, and food products. I always found it fascinating to study women and watch how they shop and walk through a store. It's insightful to watch browsers versus quick decision makers and to look at those who shop the perimeter of the store versus those who go up and down every aisle. Even understanding how women choose one particular retail location over another can open up whole new areas of consumer understanding, or in this case shopper understanding. These behaviors may have nothing to do with many parts of the demographic makeup of the target market, but a great deal to do with how women approach the shopping occasion.

Commuting to work and shopping are two examples of consumer behavior, a part of psychographics, that can offer great insight for building the experience effect.

Other psychographic behaviors include:

- Media consumption, including television shows, magazines, books, newspapers, podcasts, text messages, and websites

- Work ethic and study habits

- Social activities and hobbies

- Propensity to spend or save money

- Home improvement planning and participation

The list is endless, as you can well imagine.

These are all examples of trying to understand the target's behavior, whether it's at retail, home, work, school, or anywhere in between. When combined with thoughts and feelings, behavioral knowledge can help build a psychographic profile of the target market that can add to the demographic understanding.

We're not done yet. We can't look at demographics and psychographics once and think that we are done. It's vitally important to understand how these factors change over time:

- Are the people in the target market changing as they age? Even if the brand consistently markets to the same demographic segment (like teens), the psychographics of that segment can change over time.

- Are they shopping a certain retail outlet more frequently than ever before?

- Are they moving from urban centers to the suburbs or from the suburbs back to the urban centers in order to make specific changes in their lives?

- Are they spending more on the category than they used to or are they actually spending less?

- Are their attitudes toward spending and saving changing as a result of recent economic or political events or simply as a result of an aging demographic?

- Why are these changes happening?

Understanding trends over time can help build greater consumer understanding and help the brand experience to be continually relevant and successful. Market research trending companies have become experts in how demographic and psychographic

> *I would recommend subscribing to one of the trending services— you will be amazed at how useful the information is in building marketing programs.*

groups change over time. If the brand has the resources, I would recommend subscribing to one of the trending services—you will be amazed at how useful the information is in building marketing programs.

It's also important to understand how the target market compares to other target markets, even if there's no plan to market to others:

- Are the people in our target market likely to spend more money in each shopping trip than those in other targets do?

- Do more of our consumers work full time than those in other target markets?

- Are our consumers leaving urban centers at a faster rate than those in other target markets?

Understanding the key differences among potential targets can help build the right kind of experiences for the target. And it will also help keep those experiences distinct from those of the competition, leading to a more successful experience effect.

I think it's fair to say that most brands have a fairly good understanding of their consumers; otherwise they wouldn't be successful at all. But it's also easy to see when one brand has a far superior understanding of its consumers when compared to the average brand. Those brands that have a stellar understanding pop out in the marketplace as unusually successful.

One of those brands in my opinion is The Biggest Loser. Starting out as a reality television show, The Biggest Loser has relatively quickly become a part of pop culture and has expanded way beyond being just an entertaining show.

I bring up The Biggest Loser in this chapter because it's obvious that the brand knows its consumers inside and out. To watch people who have struggled with their weight transform themselves through proper diet, nutrition, and exercise is nothing short of inspiring—and for many it is life-changing. For the first few seasons, the reality television show was basically the entire brand. But then the website, The Biggest Loser Club, started becoming more and more important. As the brand has grown and evolved, the website has become an integral part of the experience, perhaps even more than the show itself. While the television show is still the heart and soul of the brand, the website is where all the action takes place. Those who join The Biggest Loser Club on the website can fully experience the brand. They can learn what it takes to change the way they live their lives, including how they view food and exercise. The website isn't just inspirational, though. It's educational, practical, and filled with expert advice. Consumers can learn from each other and from experts in the fields of nutrition and exercise. The balance of facts with motivation is remarkable—and right in line with what the brand's consumers need to make the necessary changes in their lives. Sound bites of the television show and website can also be followed on Twitter.

And the brand continues to expand there are now multiple books on food, cooking, and exercise, and even a soundtrack CD to use during exercise. The line of home exercise products, all branded The Biggest Loser, is also part of this incredible franchise. But what's so insightful is that the exercise products totally match the essence of the brand. The exercise products are not at all similar to the more muscle-bound brands in the exercise category.

> *Try to learn something new every day.*
> *If there's something essential that's missing in your consumer knowledge, fill in the gap with a reasonable, educated guess.*

These items are obviously uniquely created for the specific target market of the brand, and no one else. It is consumer knowledge driving the experience effect at its finest!

I highlight The Biggest Loser not necessarily for its marketing or for its particular brand experience, because in reality it has just scratched the surface of its potential. I respect the brand for its deep and intense knowledge of its consumer, which is illustrated by the empathy that it shows for those consumers who struggle with weight control and by the number of resources the brand includes to help consumers change to a healthy lifestyle. Consumers can literally join the franchise, via The Biggest Loser Club, where the brand builds an even deeper relationship and tailors its connection from consumer to consumer. It is a model relationship marketing program for any brand, let alone a brand that originated in the entertainment business. It also makes for good business since so many Americans struggle with their weight.

No brand can have this kind of deep relationship with its consumers if it doesn't understand who they are, what they need, what they want out of life, and how the brand can add value—like The Biggest Loser so clearly does. The brand has its experience effect nailed!

When all is tallied, trying to understand the consumer is a lot of work, and it often leaves marketers with almost too much information. I've seen many a client get immersed in information overload and get paralyzed as a result. It sounds odd to say, but having too much information can actually do more harm than good.

The key is not to get too caught up in the volume of information, but rather to use the information effectively. I've realized through the years that a marketer's work is never done. We can't possibly know everything there is to know about the consumer because the world is too dynamic and our research techniques are too imperfect.

Understanding consumers is a never-ending quest and a goal that is never fully reached. So you might as well enjoy the journey. Try to learn something new every day. If there's something essential that's missing in your consumer knowledge, fill in the gap with a reasonable, educated guess. You probably know a lot more about the consumer than you think, so an educated guess is better than nothing at all. It will also help to connect the seemingly random pieces of consumer understanding together to start to paint a picture of the consumer. The goal here is to define and understand the consumer in the most thorough way possible.

Try to figure out how all of this consumer information, demographic and psychographic, fits together. Start to form a picture in your mind of those in the target market, perhaps by weaving together a story about them. Introduce yourself to them and get to know them as real people.

CHAPTER **5**

Kiss a Few Babies ·
Constructing a Consumer Profile

IN THE PREVIOUS CHAPTER, we talked about understanding the target audience, the target market, consumer segments, whatever we want to call it. There may even be more than one target audience, so it's important to distinguish each consumer segment and understand as much as possible about them.

It's time now to paint a holistic picture of our consumers and to actually give them names and faces. We need to understand them more as real people, instead of just as a collection of facts. It will make building the experience effect much more real. Good marketing comes from turning theory into reality, so let's make our consumers real people, not just a collection of data.

I've seen a lot of agencies develop profiles to paint a vivid picture of consumers to see who they are and how they live their lives. To do that we need to get an even deeper understanding of how the target thinks, feels, and behaves. We need to see how these consumers live and breathe every day. We want to understand some of the thinking behind their behaviors, the reasons for their emotions, and the attitudes that motivate their decisions. Of course, we also want to incorporate what we know about them demographically as well. We need to see the whole picture, to get an understanding that

Let's make our consumers real people, not just a collection of data.

goes beyond just the demographic and psychographic observations. Then we can put it all together into a consumer profile for each target consumer. With that in hand, we will have the depth of consumer understanding we need, as well as a great tool to map out the experience effect.

There are many ways to go deeper with consumer understanding. Many of us have personally used some of the standard methodologies, like focus groups and surveys, that can generate thorough consumer learning, so I won't dwell on those approaches here. Marketers have spent hour upon hour behind the mirror in focus groups, hearing firsthand how consumers react to new product ideas, advertising concepts, website content, and package design, just to name the obvious. Marketers have also spent hundreds of hours and millions of dollars developing questionnaires for the quantitative market research testing that often follows the qualitative approach.

The classic methodology gives marketers the chance to hear input directly from the consumer and then test the learning quantitatively to make sure their observations hold true across the entire target market. Marketers can also get a good sense of the emotional versus rational drivers through this common research process, although the emotions around brand decisions are much harder to uncover. There is a somewhat standard practice that consumer marketers have been using for years that combines this kind of qualitative observational consumer learning with more quantitative consumer testing. The two techniques are designed to work in tandem but to do different things, so that together the brand has a deeper understanding of its consumers.

There are many other ways we can learn more about the consumer to go deeper with our understanding. Let's really dig into the lifestyles of our consumers.

Here are some tricks I have seen through the years that I have found to be very enlightening when trying to get to know new consumers or even in just keeping up with the ones we already know! Because most of the target markets that I have worked with have been women, it's even more important to really understand the complexity of their lives.

Read a book or go to a movie that depicts the consumer— especially a book or a movie that the target market is embracing. You'll get an incredible glimpse into their lives, their emotions, and their preferences. When I was working on Johnson's Baby Products, I was a single guy in my mid-twenties. I knew very little about babies and absolutely nothing about pregnancy. I hadn't even held a baby at that point in my life. Yet suddenly I was marketing baby products to new moms. Johnson's Baby Shampoo? I had never given a baby a bath in my life! I had a lot to learn, and I was almost as intimidated as a pregnant woman waiting for her first baby to come into her life. So like every other new-mom-to-be I read the classic book *What to Expect When You're Expecting* to see for myself what pregnant women are thinking about, worrying about, and purchasing as they go through the cycles of their pregnancy and as they make decisions for their baby's arrival. By the end of the book I still felt overwhelmed, but at least I had a sense of what a new mom might be going through. She's overwhelmed too! Of course today that same author has a website called whattoexpect.com.

Watch the television shows the target consumers watch, read their magazines, and go to the stores where they shop. You'll be amazed how much can be learned about consumers by doing what they do and by watching them while they do it. When I worked on Johnson's Baby Products, I had a lot of friends who were pregnant at the time. I would even go to their doctor's appointments just to watch the other pregnant women in the waiting room, many of whom also had newborns with them! It was quite the experience.

If you are marketing a product to a teenage girl, you can get easy access to an entire world of teen girl power just by checking out a few key television shows and reading a magazine or two. These kinds of pop culture vehicles can give an instant snapshot of the teenage girl and her life. Surf the Web where teens are navigating and interacting—an entire social networking world opens up. Go through a few Facebook pages and get an eyeful of teenage life! Trust me; I live with two of them.

Facebook is a great way to get to know consumers of all ages.

The truth is that Facebook is a great way to get to know consumers of all ages—from teenage girls to college students to adults well into their forties and fifties. I used to watch *Dawson's Creek* and *Beverly Hills 90210* religiously when I was a brand manager on Clean & Clear teen skin care at Johnson & Johnson so that I could learn about teenage girls and their lives. Of course those shows have gone off the air, and times have changed. Actually, *Beverly Hills 90210* came back with the next generation of teenagers in *90210*. It is fascinating to see how teenage lifestyles and attitudes have changed in the last decade or two—or not!

Many of these areas will not give you a full picture of the target, just a piece of it. For example, exclusively following working women on Twitter may reveal only the more tech-savvy side of the target market. But by checking out numerous venues, you can start to put together a fuller picture.

Do some detective work and also check out the competitors' marketing. See how other brands are communicating to their consumers. See if there's anything to be learned from the other brands' marketing and communications. Don't limit the investigative work to just the direct competition either. Look broadly at the brands touching the consumer and see what can be learned from them.

We can assume that many of the competitors have done a fair amount of homework, so take advantage of their research investment. Ask yourself some questions and jot down some notes:

- What are they saying to consumers? How are they saying it? What kind of language are they using?

- What claims are they making and what promises are they offering? Are there consistencies from brand to brand?

- What kinds of visuals do they use? How are they depicting the consumer?

- How does the competition depict the product or service? How do they depict the consumer using the product or service?

- What's the tone of their communications? Does it vary from brand to brand or is there a consistency here as well? Does it change for different target markets?

Look at the competitors' websites, packaging, retail displays, and advertising. See if they have a fan page on Facebook, a Twitter account, or any other online presence. Try to pull out the consumer learning they may have used to develop their communications. Compile a list of the more rational facts that the brands state as well as the emotional strings they pull. List what is common across brands and also what seems to be unique from brand to brand.

If the competitors have any kind of a consumer relationship marketing (CRM) program or loyalty club, then sign up! If the brand is in the weight loss category, then sign up for The Biggest Loser Club or Weight Watchers, for example. Start receiving the regular correspondence that the brand's loyal consumers receive. Pretend that you are one of those women trying to lose weight and experience her life.

Read the brochures front to back, and go through all the e-mails that come from the competitive brands' CRM programs. A competitive CRM program, if one exists in the category, can help you dive deeper into the learning, especially since that brand is trying to engage its consumers just like you are trying to do.

When I worked on Arm & Hammer baking soda, I got my hands on every single household cleaning product I could find. I read all the packages and all the print ads, including any of the brochures that were distributed. Back then, there was no Internet, so my options were limited! But I still captured a lot of materials and, just by going through all of my competitors' marketing materials, I got a sense of what's important to people when they clean their homes. And I kept them all on display in my office as a constant reminder that I had to do one better if my brand was going to succeed.

Now, of course, the Internet is an incredible resource. We can all find websites not only from other brands in the category, but also from advocacy groups and related organizations that are full of consumers talking and sharing their lives, their struggles, and their experiences with their favorite or not-so-favorite brands. They are debating and connecting with each other to build common bonds. It's an amazing learning opportunity for a brand manager.

Go onto the blogs and into the comments sections and listen to what people are saying. They may even be talking about your brand! They are certainly talking about things that are important to them, and that will help with your marketing. When I worked on Tylenol, I used to religiously read the reports from consumers who would call the toll-free customer service line. I would get all kinds of feedback on the promotions we were running and on the problems consumers were facing with the products. Now much of that feedback is on the Web. There are organizations you can hire to scan the world of blogs, or you can do it yourself. You'll be shocked at some of the topics that consumers are willing to talk about.

If you can swing it, spend a day with a consumer, at least one from each of the target audiences. Live with them for a day. See what they go through. Actually witness a mom's routine as she gets up, drops the kids off at school, commutes to work, makes dinner, tries to relax, and then goes to bed. Watch how she consumes media like television, magazines, direct mail, e-mail, and websites. Log on with her for an hour and see how she spends her time online. Walk in her shoes for a day and observe her as a real person. It will open your eyes; it has for me many times.

Through the years, I've spent time with medical professionals, patients, caregivers, seniors, teenagers, young kids, babies, moms, dads—you name it. It's incredibly enlightening to see how other people live and to see what they go through, particularly when we are trying to market to them, and especially when we are trying to build a relationship with them.

The more consumers I spend time with the more I realize that we are more alike than any of us think, regardless of our demographics. There are so many commonalities that bind us together, so many psychographics that we share, yet we are each individuals. Finding those similarities and those distinctions in the target audience is the key to building the right kind of experiences for them. Pulling together the common traits while identifying the individual differences is part of the magic of understanding consumers.

As we put all this learning together, we can start to paint a picture of the consumer we are targeting and develop an actual consumer profile. We'll use this profile a lot when we plan the experience effect. A consumer profile will become an invaluable tool in developing all the brand experiences we want in the marketplace.

I'd like to illustrate the concept of a consumer profile by writing out an example of how this knowledge can all start to come together. Let's create a consumer profile for a potential new furniture brand, a totally new line of furniture we will exclusively sell through our own stores, in catalogs, and on our own website. We'll assume that we've done all our homework—we've done the consumer learning that we've been talking about. We've done some qualitative and quantitative testing, read a few of the popular home improvement books, cruised through a bunch of informative websites, joined some Facebook and Google groups, and gone furniture shopping with some consumers who are in the market—some first-time buyers and some others who are more like experienced pros. We have scoured our competitors' websites and visited a few of their stores. We've even spent some time with a few retail sales representatives to observe that side of the business. Here's the good part—we've devoured all the relevant television shows on HGTV, Bravo, and the other networks.

As a brand, we have identified that an opportunity lies in being a starter furniture brand for the consumer who is becoming serious about furniture shopping. Our target consumers are not professional shoppers or interior decorators. Just for the first time in their adult lives, our consumers are getting serious about buying furniture—they've never really engaged in the process before other than to buy a piece of furniture here or there. Our brand can be there when they first seriously shop the category! Because we see a real need gap in the category, we're defining our brand as a first in a line of relatively high-quality furniture for consumers who are putting together their first real home and who are taking great pride in doing it for the first time.

The household budgets are not huge though. We are the brand that consumers can go to first to replace their current set of hand-me-downs and inexpensive substitutes. No more milk crates and unfinished bookcases here. Our brand might compete with Pottery Barn or Crate & Barrel, for example. But not Baker—it is way too high-end, too conservative, and probably in their parents' homes instead. With a pretty good, albeit hypothetical, brand definition in hand, figure 5.1 is a quick potential perceptual map to help define our brand.

FIGURE 5.1   Furniture Category Perceptual Map

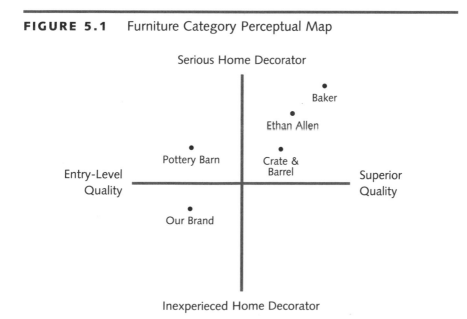

As part of our brand definition and our intense consumer learning, we have identified two high-potential consumer targets: newly married couples and successful single women. We've prioritized these two targets because we've done all our consumer work up front and we know they have unfulfilled needs we can satisfy. If we were to put celebrity faces to our consumers, it could be Ryan Reynolds and Scarlett Johansson for the newly married couple and Drew Barrymore for the single woman.

We've also determined that we have enough resources to go after these two targets and that they share enough characteristics that we can be efficient with our marketing to them, yet still appeal to each. Of course if we had hired an agency to do this, they would attach creative names to these two targets, like Nesting Lovebirds and Indies. As brand managers, we need to start putting together the experience effect, so we need to distill our consumer learning into a workable framework. Here comes the consumer profile, where we are able to actually visualize our consumers and how they live their lives.

It's not a data fest, but instead a verbal, and sometimes visual, compilation of all the information we have learned.

The consumer profile allows us to take reams of data and an abundance of loose information and put it into something we can understand. Our goal is not to oversimplify and lose meaning, but to visualize and bring clarity so that we can put it into action and use it to build the brand experience. Let's put our consumer learning to work on our new furniture brand and write out two consumer profiles, one about a newly married couple furnishing their first home together (Nesting Lovebirds) and the other about a single woman, at the moment anyway, who loves her life in the big city (Indie).

Note that in both consumer profiles, we are compiling a snap-shot of all the demographic and psychographic information we have learned, centered on the category in which we compete. It's not a data fest, but instead a verbal, and sometimes visual, com-pilation of all the information we have learned.

We are putting all the information together to depict a story about two of our potential target consumers in the furniture category.

First meet Gary and Suzette.

Gary and Suzette are both in their late twenties and have been married for just under two years now; they met in college at UCLA. While they don't yet have children, they are really starting to settle down and take root in their new home in San Mateo County, just outside of San Francisco. It's been quite a honeymoon!

They both work full time, Gary in the city at a land development firm and Suzette much closer to home as a payroll manager. With their combined income they are living quite nicely, although they are both working hard to get promoted next year.

Before they were married, they'd been living with the furniture they both had in their separate apartments, much of which was given to them by friends and family or acquired via random purchases (a chair here, a rug there). Although they started to buy pieces as they made more money together, nothing was well-thought-out or planned. Since they bought their new home six months ago, they are now ready to invest in some real furniture that better reflects the life they want to live as a couple.

Home Depot and Target are regular weekend destinations, as is Macy's on occasion. Suzette loves the bedding department there, and longs for the day when they can afford high-quality bedding for their master bedroom.

When they watch television, it tends to be just a few favorite shows throughout the week that they catch on TiVo, like *CSI Miami* or *American Idol*. Of course, the big exception is HGTV, where they pick up decorating ideas and then try to pull them off themselves. They also religiously watch the shows on Bravo, sometimes with their friends over a bottle of wine or two (although Gary would much more prefer to catch a ballgame).

Their home tends to be a central meeting place for their friends, so they want it to be stylish and comfortable. But they don't really know what that means. They like to browse for furniture and accessories, but sometimes find the actual buying process to be a drag. They shop from store to store, and from catalog to catalog, looking for just the right pieces they can afford. Sometimes they end up buying online if it's the best place to get the lowest price. Suzette is clearly the browser and ultimate decision maker, but not without running it by Gary first.

Gary and Suzette are also constantly on Facebook keeping up with friends from high school, college, and work as well as with their extended families. Suzette does a lot of research online while at work and she has been diligently picking out furniture items and making a to-do list to share with Gary. She looks through a lot of decorating magazines too. *Elle Décor* is one of her favorites, as is *Traditional Home*. Gary gets bored easily and is more likely to surf the Web while Suzette is flipping through the pages of her magazines.

It's unlikely that they will buy everything from one place since they don't really want it to look like it all matches. But it would be nice to have one place to shop and to browse where they can eventually put it all together within their budget.

Now meet Vanessa, our other target consumer.

Vanessa is a pretty typical New Yorker, not the born-and-bred type but more the kind with an acquired urban New York City style. Although she was born in Florida, she has been a New Yorker ever since she came there for work after college.

Vanessa is an independent woman living large in the city, much to the dismay of her family down south, who would rather see her married and living much closer to home. She is very successful in the real estate business despite the ups and downs in the industry.

With some extra money she made a couple of years ago, she bought a co-op apartment on the Lower East Side and has been slowly putting it together. She knows she'll probably marry someday, but for now she loves her single life and doesn't want it to change too much. While it might not be her ultimate dream home, for the first time in her life she is putting a lot of care into her investment.

Vanessa's quest for her own personal style is evident through-out the apartment, as is her active social life. The apartment is loaded with pictures of her girlfriends during their adventures around the city and the world. Whenever she travels she picks up accessories for the apartment that she just can't live without, like the rug in her living room from India and the artwork in her bedroom from Miami. But she's realizing that it's time to start buying more serious furniture that works together, particularly because she's in the business. She's active in the real estate industry, including all the websites and blogs, and she wants to start having more meetings and doing more business entertaining in her home.

Vanessa spends a lot of time working out at the gym or going out to restaurants, bars, and clubs with her girlfriends, many of whom she has met through work.

And the shopping! As soon as she sees something she likes, whether in a store or online, she grabs it, especially if it reflects her personality. Although Vanessa tends to be the trendsetter in her group, her friends, particularly the women, are constantly giving her suggestions, which sends her running to a store or to a website to find a great new blouse, a hot new song on iTunes, or the perfect accessory for her apartment. She doesn't read a lot of magazines, but she does a lot of her catching up online. Vanessa is constantly surfing the Web to keep up with the news and with her many friends around the country.

For her clothes, she tends to shop at stores like Anthropologie and J.Crew. The latest designer jeans boutiques in SoHo like True Religion or 7 For All Mankind get her through the weekends.

She's more than ready to start looking the part that she's already playing, particularly in her home.

Although these consumer profiles look a little long, they are not even fully blown out quite yet. The truth is that we could write pages of interesting material on these two sets of consumers. I've also chosen to write only one consumer profile per target, but you can and should write a few profiles for each of your targets.

No one person can represent the demographic and psychographic mixture of everyone in the target market. A few representative samples for each target market will do the trick. The more we write profiles and get to know target consumers individually, the more we start to see commonalities, which is the most interesting part. It's the magic behind combining qualitative research in focus groups with quantitative survey research—the combination of individual, anecdotal information with common traits, attitudes, and behaviors across the target.

Most important, consumer profiles help us to visualize the consumer. A consumer profile puts a face and a name to our work, and makes the consumer so much more real. I've seen marketers put actual pictures to these consumer profiles to more personally depict the lifestyle of the target market. All the better. The pictures don't have to be celebrities—the more real the better.

These consumer profiles are invaluable because they will help us to develop a more personal experience for our consumers. We can make it more real using these consumer profiles as inspiration. The point here is that a better understanding and a more personal connection make for a better brand experience.

The interesting part is that as you build the experience effect, you'll actually start to refer to your consumer profiles. You will ask yourself, "How would Vanessa respond to this advertising?" "Would Gary and Suzette find this website easy to navigate?" "What would the Nesting

What distinguishes really good marketers is a fundamental love, respect, and empathy for their consumers.

Lovebirds do?" "What would the Indies think?" You will develop such a deep understanding of your consumers that you'll start to really feel connected to them. This is what makes marketing so much more rewarding. Through the years I've noticed that what distinguishes really good marketers is a fundamental love, respect, and empathy for their consumers. The only way to develop that kind of relationship is to really get to know them—both rationally and emotionally.

CHAPTER **6**

Get Emotional

Connecting with Customers on Multiple Levels

IT'S TIME TO TALK ABOUT a critical area in marketing, a vital concept that is often neglected as marketers get immersed in developing their marketing plans. It is absolutely central to making sure that the experience effect truly connects with consumers. While it is a relatively simple concept, it is perhaps one of the easiest things to forget and one of the hardest things to put into place. Many marketers get so caught up in getting things done that they often forget a very important part of the consumer connection.

They forget the emotional side of marketing.

We've been exploring how to understand our consumers and how to build profiles to guide development of a great brand expe-

> *Many marketers get so caught up in getting things done that they often forget the emotional side of marketing.*

rience. Truly understanding our consumers is critical to building an experience for them. The experience must connect with consumers, it must get them interested, and it certainly must engage them if we are going to have a successful, sustainable brand.

We've briefly talked about how the experience must engage consumers both rationally and emotionally. Hopefully you saw the various rational and emotional elements in the consumer profiles from chapter five and in some of the examples we've already been discussing.

Let's dive even deeper into these components now, with a particular focus on the emotional side. To engage with consumers, we need to fulfill their needs, wants, and desires, both rationally and emotionally. We must communicate with them, take care of them, and add value to their lives. This has to happen on multiple levels in order to be successful.

Marketers almost always include the rational facts, but not always the emotional benefits of the brand. It's a shame because it's the emotional side that really makes the difference. The rational component is often the reason a consumer will initially look for a product—to fulfill a rational need. The consumer needs to get something done.

The emotional component, however, is why the consumer connects with the brand over time and why the brand fits into his or her life. It's why the consumer wants the brand, above and beyond why he or she needs the product and why the consumer will pay more money for a specific brand versus another one. It's also why a consumer will tell friends about the brand, and even convince them to buy it or use it too. It's why consumers will engage in a brand even though they don't need it—they want the brand anyway. It'll inspire a consumer to write a long review on Amazon.com or another website where consumers look for peer advice.

The emotional connection is how the product becomes a brand. It is certainly why any of us chooses one brand of jeans over another, even though we already have several pairs in our closet and there's no real difference between any of them. The rational component is full of facts, and the emotional component is full of feelings and lifestyle benefits. The rational side is the "what" and the emotional side is the "why," or in some cases the "why not." We all have rational needs as well as emotional wants—it's how we live our lives. A product might be able to exist without an emotional component, but a brand simply cannot.

When conducting consumer learning and market research, consumers will reveal the rational side of their needs but not always the emotional side of their wants. They will give facts and figures right away, but they may not talk about the emotions surrounding their decisions unless carefully probed. They will often say "what" they do, but they may not say "why" they do it. They may not even know why they do it, which makes it even harder to probe. As marketers, we have to dig deeper to get to the emotional side. Observing consumers' whole lives gives a glimpse into both the rational and the emotional components.

We have many of the brands in our lives because of an initial rational decision that over time turned into an emotional connection. The decisions started out as products and as they melded into our lives they became brands. What was once a rational decision over time became an emotional choice.

For me, Diet Pepsi is a good example. I drink a Diet Pepsi every single morning, the minute I get out of bed. Almost instantly. I started drinking it because I felt the need for some caffeine but just don't like the taste and temperature of regular hot coffee all that much. Diet Pepsi is an easy way for me to get some caffeine in the morning, in a way that I prefer. Rationally, Diet Pepsi helps me wake up. I'm always at the gym by 5:30 a.m., so I can use a little help getting going. Very rational, right? On the flip side though, it's very cold and fizzy, not so easy on the stomach. This should tell me that it's not a very good beverage option so early in the morning. But the fact that I drink one every single morning, and can't get started without one, is a telltale sign of an emotional connection with a brand.

That it has to be Diet Pepsi rather than any other brand of caffeinated soda is also a telltale sign! While there are rational parts to it, my Diet Pepsi routine is largely emotional. If I really think about it, the taste is nothing to write home about. A cheese omelet with peppers and onions certainly tastes a lot better. And there is tremendous speculation around the ingredients in diet sodas, which should cause anyone to think twice about it as a beverage choice.

To put it simply, I may need caffeine, but I want a Diet Pepsi. Combine my Diet Pepsi wake-up call with my Starbucks commute and I am ready for a productive day. These brand choices and intense loyalties are a complete result of my rational needs (caffeine waking me up) and emotional wants (keeping me productive)—both being met by the two brands. Consumers make these kinds of rational and emotional connections to brands all the time, like the color choices and ageless beauty of CoverGirl makeup, or the comfort and social statement of Levi's jeans.

If you think through your own life, I'm sure you could list a bunch of brands where you have made an emotional connection that may in fact overpower the rational facts of the product.

Certainly a $4.00 Starbucks cup of coffee or a $94,000 Mercedes-Benz are two great examples. Without an emotional desire for these two brands, there are certainly more rational options for consumers in these two product categories. As marketers, it is our job to make both a rational and emotional connection, at every step of our marketing plan, as part of the experience effect.

Marketers generally spend the bulk of their time and effort on the rational part, making sure they have communicated all the product features clearly so that consumers know what they are buying and can make an informed decision. They also make sure that every part of the brand experience leverages an emotional connection with consumers so that the

I'm sure you could list a bunch of brands where you have made an emotional connection that may in fact overpower the rational facts of the product.

brand is reinforced every time, whether it's the packaging, the website, collateral material, or retail environment—everything. The emotional component is just as important as the rational.

Healthcare brands put a particular emphasis on the rational side through drug claims, dosage instructions, and safety information, as well they should. They often fully communicate the rational facts about the products but leave out the emotional benefits of the brand. Many brands don't communicate how the drug will make consumers feel emotionally as well as physically, such as what the drug will do for their lives and their families or how they can take the drug every day and not feel imprisoned by a disease or a symptom. When the emotional side is portrayed, it's often in the television advertising, but not always in other parts of the brand experience, like on a website or on the packaging. The television advertising will make a dramatic emotional appeal, but then the website is relegated to lots of facts and figures, with no emotional pull at all.

Not all healthcare brands neglect the emotional side. Latisse, a prescription-only product designed to grow and thicken eyelashes, certainly portrays the emotional benefits of its brand along with the rational ones. Using Brooke Shields as their spokesperson, the advertising absolutely communicates the rational side of growing longer and thicker eyelashes, while showing people in social situations looking confident and beautiful. Brooke Shields also has a video diary online that chronicles her journey with the brand, which obviously hits even harder on the emotional side.

Latisse has done a great job of combining rational and emotional benefits as a total brand experience. But for many brands, there is a missed opportunity to truly connect with consumers when all the brand does is translate rational facts onto a marketing vehicle like a website. To make a deep connection with consumers, offer both rational and emotional benefits within the experience effect. Then consumers will truly feel the full impact of the brand, embrace it, and weave it into their lives.

Of course, to do this we really need to understand our consumers. We cannot possibly offer both rational and emotional benefits that are meaningful to our consumers if we don't understand their needs, wants, and desires. With a full profile, however, we can make a deep connection, which will translate to positive consumer behavior.

Nike is a great example of a brand that makes consistent rational and emotional connections, and I would argue that it is a successful brand as a result. In my view Nike is all about performance sportswear for athletes of all levels, something that I completely admire. Nike products offer high-tech fabrics and scientific yet fashionable designs created to deal with sweat, Mother Nature, and all the physical attributes of athletes—knees, muscles, joints, hair, etc. Nike touts these features in its advertising, on the website, and also on the product tags themselves. Its television, print, and outdoor advertising set the stage while all the other marketing elements, including online, bring the brand to life. At each point, Nike communicates what makes the products performance-related and why the product features are important to the athlete. The advertising generally shows athletes at the top of their game, or embracing extreme conditions, or even behind the scenes getting ready for the action, with the help of high-performance footwear and clothing. There are no specific claims or details in the television advertising; that's all left for the website or the clothing tags at retail, where full descriptions of materials and workmanship are provided. For example, Nike.com is loaded with specific product details that reinforce the advertising communication as you navigate around the site.

Not with the same level of detail each time, and not always in words, but always consistently, the brand tells the rational side of the Nike story. It tries to make a rational connection with the consumer as part of the experience effect—like the Nike Clima-FIT convertible running jacket made for running in the winter that I read about on their website. Smart. But there's an emotional component communicated as well. As a consumer, I get the sense that these product features will make me a better athlete, make me more of an athlete. I want to believe that these product features will somehow make me fitter, younger, tougher, cooler, even though in reality none of that is necessarily true—it's all very emotional. The brand doesn't literally tell me that. But through the imagery, language, and tone, I'm left with that emotional impression. It's all a part of the experience effect under the theme of "Just Do It," because I really can do it just like the athletes who endorse the brand. My takeaway is that Nike will in fact make me feel just a little bit fitter, younger, tougher, and cooler. Sure, that jacket I read about on the website and then bought for running will protect me from the elements, a very rational benefit. But will Nike make me fitter, younger, tougher, cooler? Literally no, but emotionally yes. What counts is that I believe that it might—and I want to believe that it will. And because I want to believe, in my mind it becomes true. Nike reinforces my beliefs with every piece of marketing. Because I believe in Nike and in that running jacket, I run

> *Will Nike make me fitter, younger, tougher, cooler? Literally no, but emotionally yes.*

every week of the year, regardless of the weather, even on days when it's raining. And when I'm running in the rain, I wear this cool matte silver jacket that keeps me from getting cold. Because I'm comfortable and can keep running even though it's cold and rainy, I continue to stay fit, which keeps me just a little bit younger. In my view, the emotional benefits of Nike are probably more important than the rational ones, although for me one doesn't exist without the other. So when I go to a retail store like Dick's Sporting Goods to buy my running gear, I really do read the tags and I often end up spending more money than I had planned. Of course, Dick's Sporting Goods has a Nike section where the merchandise is well displayed, with pictures of weekend warriors. My brand perceptions are reinforced once again with a consistent point-of-purchase experience. And have you been to one of the Niketown flagship stores? Wow, talk about an inspirational athletic experience as you shop through the various departments organized by sport. You can demo the latest tools of the trade, available exclusively right then and there, all surrounded by life-size portraits of the athletes who endorse the products, many of them featuring their own limited-edition sportswear.

The emotional component to Nike is what drives my loyalty, and it's why I have the sneakers, the shorts, some shirts, a few of the sweatpants, and a hat or two. I buy the whole lot, every time I buy, whether I'm running, working out, skiing, or playing tennis. The Nike experience drives my loyalty and my behavior, and I've incorporated Nike into my life.

Every time and everywhere I am in contact with the Nike brand, my needs and wants are fulfilled over and over again, consistently. Nike has done an exemplary job of making sure that the rational and emotional components both are complete and consistent with every facet of the brand experience. The brand provides the technical details of the products that I need to know to make good choices and combines them with an athletic high that I know I'll get when I actually use them in my sport of choice. With every single Nike product and every single Nike brand communication, I know what Nike is and I know what I will experience.

To put it simply, I may need running gear, but I want Nike.

Nike is not the only example. It's possible to create both rational and emotional connections and benefits for consumers in every single category, for any brand. Some may be easier than others, but if we look hard we can uncover both sides. Try to find a category where that is not possible!

To illustrate, let's list some categories and try to outline possible rational and emotional benefits (see figure 6.1).

We could obviously go on and on. While these examples are hypothetical, rational and emotional benefits exist in any category. We just have to uncover and leverage them.

Consumers in every category have rational needs and emotional wants. Our job as marketers is to unleash the power of these components and merge them together with our knowledge of the consumer and with what we can offer as a brand. All that happens with the experience effect.

We need to create both a rational and emotional connection to consumers as part of the experience effect. Give consumers the

FIGURE 6.1   Examples of Rational and Emotional Benefits

Category	Rational Benefit (Need)	Emotional Benefit (Want)
Kids' cereal	Nutrition	Fun breakfast
Fruits and vegetables	Vitamins and minerals	Look and feel better
Cookies	Satisfy hunger	Provide comfort
Deodorant	Control odor	Feel like a man or woman
Hair color	Cover gray	Stay young and sexy
Toothpaste	Prevent cavities	Prevent embarrassment
Cars	Get to work	Get noticed
Pens	Sign documents	Security from identity theft
Pillows	Support posture	Reflect personal style
Computers	Send correspondence	Connect with friends

facts and the product attributes they need so they can make a rational decision about the product benefits. But also give them the emotional connection they want in their lives. We don't have to necessarily tell consumers the emotional part specifically in words, but rather show them the emotional benefit they will gain by incorporating the brand into their lives.

The key is to do it consistently across each of the brand's touchpoints. With our intense knowledge of our consumers in hand, it's time to start mapping out the potential touchpoints where we can engage with them.

CHAPTER 7

Reach Out and Touch

Mapping Effective and Engaging Touchpoints

IN CHAPTERS FOUR, FIVE, AND SIX we've been exploring the need for a full and deep understanding of our consumer targets. Understanding our consumers and their rational and emotional needs is critical to developing the experience effect.

A deep understanding is the foundation for making a connection with our consumers and motivating their behavior, perhaps even adding value to their lives—which is ultimately what we need to do as marketers if we hope to build a relationship with them and if we hope to build brand loyalty to any extent.

Now it's time to do what we set out to do: actually create the experience effect. We now not only have a good understanding of the target markets, both rationally and emotionally, but we've also defined the brand. We've got what we need to start building. The next step in our process here is the touchpoint.

Marketers use a lot of different terms when it comes to describing consumer touchpoints. Some use terms such as *media, channels, vehicles, venues, connections,* or even *engagements.* All of these terms mean the same thing in my mind. I like the concept of a touchpoint because it is so visually descriptive and so broad in its potential coverage. It's a chance for the brand to reach out, make a connection, provide information, and motivate consumers to do something that will ultimately impact their lives.

> *A touchpoint is anything that puts the brand within arm's reach of a consumer—movie theaters, cell phones, bathroom stalls, chat rooms—anything and everything.*

Marketers have often thought of touchpoints in only the traditional way, as in television and print advertising. In a constantly changing world of media options, I'd like to think of touchpoints in the broadest way possible to include any channel available to us, whether on the Internet, out of home, in any kind of mail, or in any manner in which the brand can connect with a consumer. Any opportunity to reach a consumer is a touchpoint that we should potentially use to build the brand experience. It can be anything that puts the brand within arm's reach of a consumer. Movie theaters, cell phones, bathroom stalls, chat rooms, exercise bikes at the gym, taxicabs, pens, banner ads, freight trucks, social media—anything and everything.

Don't be constrained by traditional thinking, like television advertising or even websites (the "new traditional"). Think even broader than what is currently called the new media on the Internet, like Facebook, LinkedIn, or Twitter. With the proliferation of media options, the list of potential touchpoints is almost endless. Almost anything is a possibility—even people walking up and down the streets, one of the oldest forms of media, although now we call them "street teams."

Banana Republic does a great job of using shopping bags as a touchpoint. If there's a sale happening at Banana Republic, then the streets and the mall are filled with consumers carrying shopping bags announcing the sale.

Touchpoints themselves can have rational and emotional components. Advertising touchpoints can be pretty straightforward, but the creative execution can certainly leverage an emotional connection—an entire industry has been built around it. I do love the newer media and the more creative touchpoints for their emotional component. Many of our choices here have strong emotional potential, especially in areas where consumers can connect with each other and share their experiences, like in blogs, message boards, forums, or the social networking sites like MySpace, LinkedIn, Facebook, or Twitter. These touchpoints are hugely emotional and offer a tremendous opportunity for marketers if we engage with consumers correctly. Of course, user-generated content within a touchpoint hits the top of the emotional chart. Just take a look at some of the videos that consumers submit to websites about breast cancer, for example.

YouTube is a multiple touchpoint for advertising and sponsorship opportunities in addition to the video uploads. For some brands, it makes sense to specifically develop long-format advertising for use on YouTube alone, and a lot of brands are adding their advertising to YouTube as a way to work around DVR and TiVo surfing. Nike actually puts extended versions of its advertising on YouTube so that brand lovers can get the full experience. Kraft uploads how-to videos from its website as well. So as a consumer you may not catch the television advertising when scheduled but you can still experience it online. The rules are less stringent and the emotions can run much higher, which means the brand can go much deeper with consumers than it can on network television advertising. The videos don't get skipped as much since the consumer is viewing by choice, but be prepared for all the user-generated comments. The experience is quite engaging.

Some touchpoints are purchased, like television, magazine, or newspaper advertising. For other touchpoints, such as a blog or forum, a brand needs to be invited in or be invited to stay in once it enters. We call this the difference between paid and earned media.

Touchpoints can be static, like a flat outdoor billboard that consumers pass as they drive along a highway, or they can be much more interactive, like a live-action display with a mobile text-in option, where consumers can ask for more information or join a loyalty club. Notice the difference in the depth of the brand experience between these two touchpoints.

Some touchpoints have been highly controversial, often when a marketer uses them for the first time. When movie theater advertising first broke, many moviegoers were up in arms because they had paid to relax at a theater only to be bombarded by advertising. Now movie theater advertising is the norm and more acceptable to the consuming public, although you may have noticed that the entertainment value of the advertising has greatly increased, partly because marketers had to earn their way into the touchpoint in order to be accepted. The brands had to create a better experience to make the proper connection with consumers. At this touchpoint, brands have to add value to the consumer movie experience to get noticed, and marketers can do that in the theater by bringing entertainment—particularly while moviegoers are waiting for the main attraction. Much of movie theater advertising has become creatively spectacular, in long-format telling a ministory, almost as prep to the movie itself. When coupled with product placement in the movie itself, this is a smart way to use a touchpoint and is also apparently effective in many product categories. Otherwise we wouldn't see brands continually use it.

Advertising on the movie theater screen is not the only touch-point at a movie theater complex. There is also the popcorn bag; Calvin Klein jeans was one of the first brands to use popcorn bags at movie theaters as a touchpoint. It felt so radical at the time, but it's just another way to reach out to consumers, like anything else. It is a touchpoint that is literally an arm's length away from the consumer! There is also the concession stand itself, posters on the way into the theater, outdoor space around the theater, and the bathroom stalls in the building. And that's not even really thinking that hard. Not to mention the online purchasing systems to avoid lines and get tickets in advance.

As I mentioned, some touchpoints can generate a lot of controversy. Bathroom stalls may very well be one of them. I recently saw a poster for Lotrimin Ultra in the bathroom at my gym, and I thought to myself, "That's a great use of a touchpoint!" It was literally right next to the stall. A little gross, but really effective! Often when a marketer tries something new that is intrusive in consumers' lives, it generates controversy. Chat rooms and blogs where marketers go in uninvited or unannounced are cause for some controversy, and perhaps rightly so, although truthfully, some of that controversy is more about how a marketer uses a touchpoint than about the touchpoint itself.

> *Often when a marketer tries something new and is intrusive in consumers' lives, it generates controversy.*

As good marketers, we have a responsibility to use a touchpoint with care, with true honesty, and with the utmost of ethical behavior as it relates to consumers' lives. We need to be respectful that we are entering their lives, and we should not interrupt our consumers unless we can add value, unless we are invited, or unless consumers can close us out if they so choose. At the very least we should enter only if consumers have the option of ignoring the brand without fear of retribution. Stalking is out of the question! This issue comes up a lot in healthcare marketing, whether on a prescription, an over-the-counter brand, or a health and beauty aid brand, where personal issues and privacy concerns are real. With pharmaceuticals it is a legal requirement to respect consumer privacy, but in all marketing it should be a normal course of ethical business.

Consumers may not want a direct-mail piece coming to the house announcing their personal health issues on the outside of the envelope (another touchpoint). Who would want the postal carrier and neighbors to know? Or consumers may not want employers to see personal e-mails about a health concern either (yet another touchpoint). Who would want their employer questioning their ability to get the job done?

We owe our consumers the privacy and respect they deserve, no matter what brand we are marketing. Regardless of the category or the information we are communicating, we need to interact with consumers on their terms. Allow them to engage if they want to engage, and always give them the option to disengage with no recourse.

E-mail spam is an extreme example (but yet another touchpoint). If you are like me, your e-mail inbox is flooded every day with spam. Legitimate marketers first ask for an opt-in and then always give the option to opt out. Illegitimate marketers don't do any of that. They just keep the spam coming, over and over again, through different versions of the same e-mail, regardless of the request to stop and regardless of the spam filters in place.

Spam marketers prey on the unsuspecting and count on repetition to break through. And in many ways, they destroy the e-mail touchpoint for the respectful marketers, the vast majority of us. It is our duty to treat every touchpoint and every consumer with the kind of respect that we would want in return.

So how do you know when you've got a touchpoint on your hands? Simple: If there's an opportunity to interact with a consumer (respectfully), you have a potential touchpoint. Some are easy to detect, as we've been discussing. Others require a little more creativity. But the easiest way to discover a touchpoint is to see how consumers live their lives.

> *If there's an opportunity to interact with a consumer (respectfully), you have a potential touchpoint.*

Remember the consumer learning and consumer profiles in chapters four and five? Here's where they come in to good use again! Follow consumers for a day, a week, or even a month, and discover with your own eyes all their touchpoints. Live their lives and observe. See what they do as they go about their days, as they commute to work, drop off the kids at school, spend time online, and go out to lunch. Observe the difference between a weekday and a weekend. Watch the media they consume and the touchpoints where they interact. As we sort through the various touchpoints, we can start to segment those that are easily accessible as marketers versus those that are a little more complex. There are touchpoints that are paid media, meaning there is a partner who owns the space and will sell it in an established, formal way, like television advertising. Others are paid for in that there is a cost to develop them, like a website. And then there are earned media touchpoints that are a little more underground, most likely free or of little cost, that are certainly still a legitimate way to connect with consumers.

Use the entire consumer learning we did in chapter five, but pay particular attention to ways and places where the brand can touch consumers. The consumer profiles we spoke about in chapter five will certainly provide a good start. Now take that profile and trace out the consumer's behavior throughout the day.

Literally map out a day in the life of the consumer, and list all the touchpoints. You will be amazed at how many you can identify pretty easily.

Think about a working mom, as an example. Perhaps this particular working mom lives in the suburbs of a major metropolitan area and commutes into the city for work. Let's say she has two children and works full time, commuting an hour each way to work. If we were to follow her throughout her day, any typical day, we could easily list a whole range of touchpoints. We can list all the opportunities where as marketers we could reach out to her and invite her into our brand. We won't worry about which brand or category for now; let's just make a laundry list of potential touchpoints. We will figure out later if they make sense or if we can afford them. Open up the mind creatively!

Some of the touchpoints for a working mom might be:

- Early morning television, like *The Today Show* or one of the news programs on CNN.

- The physical newspaper is not quite dead yet, although it is quickly being replaced by online news sources, including those with mobile applications. Commuters on public transportation, like our working mom, still rely heavily on newspapers, although this may be dwindling. Look at how Kindle is attempting to replace the physical book.

- Product packaging of the brands she has incorporated into her morning routine. Some are obvious, like the large back panel on a breakfast cereal box. Some are not so obvious, like toothpaste, makeup, shampoo, diapers, etc. And not just during the morning routine, either. Consumers interact with packaging all day long, across a huge range of categories and industries.

- Drive time radio in the car and outdoor advertising on the commute to work. Outdoor advertising can be roadside billboards, public transportation (including the stations, buses, trains, subways), posters at construction sites, anything outside.

- Satellite radio. Yes, even this industry is allowing marketers to participate now, despite the initial no-advertising sales pitch to consumers. It might be more about a marketing sponsorship than about advertising, but it's still a touchpoint no matter what we call it. A brand can also influence editorial content on much of the programming.

- Brochures and products in the day-care center where she drops off the kids.

- Mobile devices used all day long, whether a cell phone, iPhone, or BlackBerry.

- Common areas at work such as the cafeteria or the break room where employees grab a quick breakfast or conduct impromptu meetings with colleagues. Touchpoints here can include the coffee cups, napkins, tray covers, signage, and even the vending machines.

- Web homepages like Yahoo, where people check personal c-mail and catch up on a few issues. More and more consumers are customizing their homepages, and thereby allowing only certain information from certain sources into their lives. As a brand, if you can add value at this level with consumers, then this is a great touchpoint.

- Search engines like Google—for both paid and natural search—are a basic requirement as a touchpoint if a brand wants to connect with consumers during their online activity. They can often be the beginning of an online experience.

- E-mail sent from brands, received either at work, at home, or both.

- Banner ads on websites visited. Have you seen how creative these little buggers are getting?

- Websites themselves, branded and unbranded, where rich content is featured and connections are made. Banner advertising and sponsorships are obvious, but there are many other ways to influence content as marketers.

- E-mail signatures. Yes, even an e-mail signature can say something about a brand and should therefore be given consideration.

- Company press releases and statements picked up by the press—these often make it into editorial content, both online and offline, and when a consumer reads about it as news, it's another touchpoint.

- Chat rooms, blogs, and social networking groups where consumers interact with each other and generate content themselves.

- Books, pencils, pens, tissue boxes. Pharmaceutical companies are famous for these touchpoints, although they have recently been removed as options for prescription brands unless they are medically relevant. Other categories like over-the-counter drugs and certainly local businesses like real estate or insurance agents still use these touchpoints.

- Common areas (including bathrooms) in public places like shopping malls, office parks, etc.

- Employer intranet sites, if you can get onto them legitimately.

- Doctor's office waiting room and examination rooms. Brochures, posters, interactive displays, videos, etc. I've even seen brand messaging on the disposable paper that protects the examination tables, and not just from pharmaceutical companies.

- Retail store displays, circulars, in-store radio, couponing machines, all at the point of purchase. Wal-Mart has a tremendously powerful in-store television network, as do other retailers. Some even have their own in-store radio programming. Think Starbucks with its own music selections/compilations and Best Buy retail radio with Ryan Seacrest as host. Even graphic posters on the floors have made their way into grocery and drugstore aisles.

- Retail bags, bag inserts, and the coupons that get printed out at the register along with the pharmaceutical drug information from the pharmacy.

- Couponing and rebates via Sunday newspapers, direct mail, online, etc. Like the point of purchase touchpoint, there's an entire industry built around couponing—the complexity is amazing if you've never been exposed to it.

- Receptionists, greeters, any form of customer service personnel. After all, they are the literal face of the brand. I'll be talking about customer service personnel more in chapter eight.

- Direct mail. Believe it or not, some brands still use the traditional mailbox, or snail mail. The industry calls these kinds of marketing programs consumer relationship marketing (CRM). Direct marketing or CRM is both online and offline and is multifaceted in its potential touchpoints; there are dozens of ways to reach the consumer via a CRM program, whether it's through a brochure in the mail or a link to a website sent via e-mail. Even Twitter can be part of a CRM program now. Don't forget the monthly bill (e-mail or snail mail) if that's relevant for the brand—even that is a touchpoint.

- Magazines, both online and offline. Not only for their advertising potential, but also for the opportunity to place products and influence editorial.

- Prime time and even late night television when the work day is through. Perfect for the insomnia category.

- Online television sites like Hulu.com. I now personally watch most of my favorite television shows on demand. I'm sure that many a working mom does exactly the same, as viewing on these channels continues to grow exponentially.

- Online entertainment and gaming sites. Be careful here about editorial content and the brand's proximity to controversy. But if the entertainment is appropriate, go for it.

- Shopping mall. The shopping mall is like a buffet of touchpoints. Next time you're there, see if you can count all the possible touchpoints. Signage, video, shopping bags, customer service personnel, kiosks, you name it.

There are also a number of custom brand or themed events at shopping malls that generate great participation. The mall has gotten just as rich as the grocery store for its potential touchpoints, not to mention what a brand can do with its packaging and point of purchase materials in the stores themselves.

- Lest we forget, Facebook and Twitter. The brand can have a presence here, but so do the employees who manage the brand. Now that many employees have Facebook pages and Twitter accounts, the lines are blurring around personal privacy and brand marketing. Particularly for customer service employees and senior management, content on Facebook and Twitter can reinforce (or destroy) the brand's experience effect. If a senior member of a company is using foul language or parading his or her extravagant social life on one of these social media sites, it is sure to impact the consumers' perceived brand experience. I've also seen many employees complain about their job on their status updates, which certainly gives me a perception of that company and even its brands.

Okay, enough already; no need to beat this to death! The list can literally go on and on and can get more and more detailed with greater knowledge of the consumer. The better the consumer profile and the more we know about the consumer, the longer the potential list.

We crafted this list thinking about a working mom as our consumer, although truthfully it would fit for a lot of different consumer profiles. But be careful not to overgeneralize. The point of the exercise is to think about the specific consumer for the brand

and list his or her specific touchpoints. The list for a working mom is likely to be different from the list for an older woman or for a teenage girl for that matter, although there is certainly some common ground. Remember that demographics alone do not make up the entire consumer profile. The list of touchpoints also varies based on day of the week, time of year, etc. Think about the entire demographic and psychographic profile of the consumer when listing the potential touchpoints.

Online behavior is one psychographic element that is much more telling than most demographic elements, at least when constructing a list of potential touchpoints.

Notice how there is a complete mix of high-cost and low-cost options, as well as a mix of more traditional media with more innovative forms. Many of those touchpoints can be customized and segmented for target markets, while some are more mass in nature. Keep in mind that even mass vehicles can also be customized to some extent. Certainly for television advertising, for example, targeting can be done by choosing the programming content, network, time of day, and region of the country. Advertising customization can happen both online and offline, where the list of vehicles, including cable channels and website options, is almost as long as the list of potential touchpoints themselves. Many other forms of paid media can be targeted and customized for the consumer as well.

We are not yet ready to decide which touchpoints are the most useful and most valid for what we are trying to accomplish. We are just brainstorming the entire potential list. Be open and creative.

Back in chapter two, I mentioned my loyalty to Marriott hotels as a business traveler. If the marketers of Marriott were to follow the process we've been describing, they could easily map out my potential touchpoints as a busy business traveler. Marriott could brainstorm a list, like we just did for a working mom, if the marketers followed me for a day, or a week, or even a month. Marriott would find that I watch a few minutes of early morning television, that I'm on my iPhone all day long, and that I read my news headlines on Yahoo as I check my e-mail throughout the day. They could follow both my personal and work life to witness the different touchpoints. They would know that I have two e-mail accounts, one for work and one for personal use, and they could figure out how best to reach me, given that I have positioned the brand as servicing my workplace needs. They would know that I sometimes walk to work and sometimes commute on the train, which exposes me to very different touchpoints. They would know what airports and highways I frequent because of my travel schedule. They would also know that I spend a lot of time in the car on the weekends and that I get most of my entertainment online, including music, television shows, and movies. I bring a lot of that entertainment via a mobile device with me to the gym and on the train as I go to work. The brand managers could easily figure out what trade publications I read, both online and offline, and they could go to the business seminars I frequent every year.

Using me as a prototypical business consumer, Marriott could build my consumer profile and map out all my touchpoints, ultimately to construct an experience for me. Marriott could literally map out my day and the days of other business travelers to see how the brand could connect with me. The brand managers could make a long list of my potential touchpoints

> *By understanding consumers and mapping out all their potential touchpoints, we are well on our way to creating a well-thought-out experience effect.*

and prioritize them based on the ones that make the most sense. Although it may seem like a laundry list at this point, by understanding consumers and mapping out all their potential touchpoints, we are well on our way to creating a well-thought-out experience effect. We are on the path to building a marketing plan that will connect the brand to its consumers in their lives, engaging them and adding value where it counts most.

Now that we know what touchpoints are and have a list of options, we can talk about how we activate them.

CHAPTER 8

Squishees from Kwik-E-Mart
Activating Touchpoints

WE ARE NOW GETTING to the crux of the experience effect—actually mapping out the touchpoints and putting them into action. It's time to bring the marketing plan and the experience effect to life, and we are hitting some critical ground in the process. It's critical work because as marketers we now have to make choices about how to reach our consumers.

As we mapped out the potential touchpoints in chapter seven, it became apparent that there are lots of places to interact with consumers. Too many in fact. We now have to decide which touchpoints are the most important for our consumer and which ones make the most sense for our brand. Then ultimately we need to decide how to put the touchpoints to work, uniquely yet consistently each time. Basically, we need to choose the right touchpoints and then we need to activate them.

Deciding which touchpoints are the most important comes from truly understanding the consumers and how the brand fits within their lives. We will want to interact with consumers when it is the most appropriate so that our marketing resources are at their most efficient.

Thinking back to the Marriott example might help illustrate the point. Marriott is my choice for business travel. If the brand were to use me as an example to map consumer touchpoints and to decide which ones to activate, then it would need to understand me as a business traveler. And as they map out my touchpoints, the brand managers need to activate ones that will reach me when I am most receptive to communication about my business travel needs. This would probably not be when I am relaxing on the weekend or running my kids around to their activities. If they were to hit me with a message at that point, I would likely ignore it. But if Marriott connects with me during the business week, when I am commuting to work, for instance, then the brand has a chance to not only reach me, but to fully engage me. At this point I may be more willing to experience the brand. Work is on my mind at this point, and if luck were to have it, I may even be figuring out my travel schedule for the week.

This is perfect timing to send a targeted communication to a receptive consumer who has a need at that moment in time—at that touchpoint. The timing is perfect to send an e-mail to my work account with a link to the brand website, to tell me about the multitude of city locations (rational benefit) and about the attentive service and customized options through the Marriott Rewards program (emotional benefit). At this point the brand has a better chance of sealing the deal for my next business trip with a reservation at a Marriott hotel using my Marriott Rewards membership number. To reach me as a business traveler, the brand could also use drive time radio or transit advertising as perfect touchpoints to engage me. Providing me with an app for my cell phone would also be an ideal touchpoint choice for Marriott. Since I am a loyal consumer, the brand could also give me an incentive to follow it on Twitter to even further advance customer service.

The best touchpoints are the ones that can get incorporated into consumers' lives at the time when it makes the most sense for the brand. For me with Marriott, it's when I'm making choices about business travel. This is just a personal example meant to illustrate a very important point. One of the keys to a successful experience effect is to match up the potential touchpoints outlined for the brand with knowledge about the consumer. It actually won't be hard to do if we've done all the right homework.

> *The best touchpoints are the ones that can get incorporated into consumers' lives at the time when it makes the most sense for the brand.*

At this point, it's a relatively easy exercise of matching like for like. In the Marriott example, matching business communications with likely business touchpoints couldn't be simpler, although admittedly the devil is in the details. The part that could be a little trickier is making sure that the touchpoints make sense not only for the consumer but also for the brand. But if we've done the right homework as discussed in chapter three, where we defined the brand, then this won't be hard either. All the brand definition work is going to come in handy here. We know the brand and what it stands for, and we created its distinct personality. So match up the touchpoints outlined for the consumer by picking the ones that also make sense coming from the brand. Activate only those touchpoints that work within the brand definition and that make sense to engage the consumer.

On the laundry list of touchpoint possibilities, weed out the ones that don't make sense for the brand, even if it's a touchpoint where the brand could interact with the consumer. Pick the ones that make the most sense for the brand! Don't pick a highly technical touchpoint if the consumer is not tech-savvy, for instance. If the brand is serious, it might not make sense to pick a touchpoint that is too frivolous. If the brand holds a specific place in the category, pick touchpoints that exist in that same kind of space.

Movie marketing provides a great case study of what I'm talking about here. Notice that every time a major movie comes out, the studios activate what is probably a pretty standard set of touchpoints to generate awareness about the movie release. There are mass media touchpoints like television, magazine, newspaper, and outdoor advertising, and online touchpoints like websites and banner ads as well as content generated for blogs and message boards. Movies are often promoted on highly targeted banner ads that appear on instant messenger windows where the trailer can be viewed by clicking on the link, or often the movie can be "friended" on MySpace or Facebook. When the targeting is done right, it can be an effective way to drive viewership of the trailer and early box office results. The studios of course dominate the talk shows, entertainment programming, and movie review shows (online and offline) for the entire time prior to the release. Pay even closer attention and look at the context of all those touchpoints. The selection of touchpoints, when done well, matches the target consumer for the movie. Movies marketed to teenagers are featured in touchpoints where teenagers are hanging out with their friends, often online on social networking sites, but also in physical locations like kiosks and bold signage at the mall. Action-adventure movies are marketed in places where the movie studio can connect with men, romantic comedies with women, etc.

Other product categories can learn from this established movie marketing protocol. The studios also match the personality of the film with the personality of the touchpoint. A serious drama starring Meryl Streep will utilize touchpoints that not only will reach women, but will also reach them with the right tone and manner, like on *Oprah* or on iVillage.com. An action-adventure film starring Hugh Jackman will utilize touchpoints that will connect with men when they are in the right mindset, like on websites about sports and travel rather than on those about work and fatherhood.

A relatively recent but now classic movie marketing example of matching brand personality with touchpoint activation is the release of *The Simpsons Movie.* The film was a blockbuster despite a concern that consumers might not pay cash to see an entertainment property that is readily accessible on television. Of course those who didn't want to shell out the cash simply waited for the cable release, which was also a huge success.

It's been said that one of the keys to the film's opening weekend triumph was the promotion with the convenience store 7-Eleven. Prior to the film's release, 7-Eleven reinvented a dozen of its stores by renaming them to reflect the infamous convenience store Kwik-E-Mart from *The Simpsons* television show.

The promotional stores exclusively offered products that matched content from the film, like Squishees. Of course if you are a fan of *The Simpsons* then you know that the 7-Eleven knockoff is a regular part of the plot, although even nonviewers know that much of the show has become a part of pop culture—even "d'oh!" is in *Webster's New American Dictionary*! Although this promotion was in only a dozen stores, the promotion smartly activated a series of public relations stories in entertainment television shows, online sites, and magazines for weeks prior to the movie's release. More touchpoints! Even trade publications picked up the innovative marketing as a story line, which helped to fuel the pre-release buzz. More touchpoints! All this hype, completely consistent with the brand, was generated from only a dozen promotional retail locations—but the buzz helped to fuel the movie's opening weekend box office success. Some call this merely good public relations, but I think of it as well-coordinated, great marketing.

This example from *The Simpsons Movie* represents the epitome of using touchpoints that match the brand and match the consumer, with parallel tonality. And it also represents how one effective touchpoint can launch a whole bunch more. Using a touchpoint that completely matched an element of the brand's character and personality was an innovative, bold, and striking move for the movie studio. I'm sure it was an expensive promotion, but it clearly helped to drive box office success. It completely engaged the property's fan base and even grabbed casual fans like me. Ten years of fan anticipation didn't hurt either.

Notice that we don't have to activate the entire laundry list of touchpoints, just the ones that are the best match.

When we activate touchpoints that leverage both consumer understanding and brand definition, then the truth is we don't have to utilize all that many of them. A few really effective touchpoints may be all we need, or all we can afford for that matter. A dozen retail locations for *The Simpsons Movie* certainly worked. Notice that we don't have to activate the entire laundry list of touchpoints, just the ones that are the best match. Still a lot of work, no doubt, even with just a handful of touchpoints. The creation of advertising and the development of a website alone are enough for several full-time marketing jobs. Now try to activate the newer or more innovative touchpoints and our resources are likely to run out! The key is to understand the resources on the team, both money and people, and allocate them to the touchpoints that make the most sense.

It may be an exaggeration, but it certainly feels like media proliferation is at an all-time high. However, the truth is that there have been new media options constantly being introduced and we have always felt like we didn't know enough about them. I don't think this time period is all that different; it's just developing at a faster pace. It is true that the digital revolution has opened up all new avenues for marketers to engage consumers and for consumers to connect with each other. New options are coming at us constantly. But just because the touchpoint is new and just because it feels ever-present does not mean that we have to use it for the brand. I frequently tell clients not to go digital just for digital's sake and to use social media when it makes sense for the brand and for the consumer. Even if social media does make sense, then the question quickly becomes how to use it to be consistent with the experience effect.

The digital world is indeed the new medium at the moment, and it's exciting. But that doesn't mean that all of it makes sense for every brand and every consumer at every moment. Let the brand definition and the consumer profile guide the decisions.

I do believe that for most brands, some kind of digital experience, when done appropriately, makes sense to engage consumers. Certainly a website and e-mail communication have become almost a cost of doing business. Be mindful of the brand and of the consumer and methodically determine if other digital touchpoints make sense for the brand. Then decide how to use these touchpoints, like any of the others, rather than just going digital for digital's sake. There is no point in being on Twitter if the brand doesn't use it appropriately or if the consumer isn't there. As we think through what's best for the consumer and for the brand, we should now be prioritized down to a handy set of realistic touchpoints that we want to activate. Budget aside, we've done all the hard thinking and have made many of the hard choices.

I say budget aside because we might not be able to afford all the touchpoints we've chosen to activate, but that depends completely on the size of the business and the size of the marketing budget. Budgeting is a lot of work in and of itself, so don't take it lightly. Get some help here. If we prioritize the touchpoints we've selected based on their effectiveness at engaging consumers and based on a match with the brand definition, then the budget process will be a lot easier. The list will be a lot shorter, and it will naturally be somewhat prioritized.

For the sake of this discussion, we'll assume that we have our prioritized list of touchpoints completed and that they all fit within the budget. The experience effect is all about building consistent brand experiences from touchpoint to touchpoint. Now is the time for us to bring the effect to fruition. Consistency is the key to good marketing and to the experience effect.

This is where many marketers fall down on the job—the execution kills them. As they start to roll out their marketing plan, whether they call it the experience effect or not, they do not keep the experience consistent from touchpoint to touchpoint. All the great plans fall down when the execution isn't consistent with the brand and with other executions. The experiences are often scattered and all over the map, which means that the branding is all over the map as well. Consumers may end up experiencing different brands at each touchpoint because there is little or no consistency.

With the experience effect, consumers know the brand; they know they are getting what they need and want from the brand, and they are enjoying the brand each and every time, consistently. We all know what happens when the experiences are not consistent.

Let's take a look at Verizon. The brand is an all-encompassing provider of home and cell phone service, Internet access, and cable television for both business and residential customers. Or at least I think that's what the brand offers. Not just wireless, but all consumer needs in phone, Internet, and television. The website and the brand's brochures promise flawless service and all the benefits of combining phone, Internet, and television, as opposed to buying the products separately from different companies. The brand promises better service from one-stop shopping with an integrated network, with the best and most comprehensive coverage available.

The television advertising for Verizon is arguably the best in the industry and perhaps the most memorable too. Highly recognizable and clear as a bell, it is loaded with claims and promises that consumers want to hear. Become a Verizon customer, though, and the actual experience doesn't exactly match the brand promise.

Sure, the wireless coverage is as good as promised. But the comprehensive, bundled service? Inconsistent. The monthly bill is a confusing mess with mystery charges that appear to come out of nowhere. I defy anyone to truly understand the monthly fees from service to service. The benefits of bundled services as promised on the website are nowhere to be found on the bill. The advertising touchpoint is in no way consistent with the monthly billing touchpoint.

Try to get a customer service representative on the phone who can help with the multiple services—these people don't seem to exist, at least after several attempts and literally hours on the phone trying to connect with one. This is completely inconsistent with the promise of the Verizon bundled packages.

Some Verizon Wireless stores are packed with customers, again waiting for an unreasonably long time to be serviced by employees who may or may not know the features and benefits of the product line. Sometimes the service is as amazing as promised, and sometimes it's exasperating.

> Consumers are not surprised by poor service, so they have relatively low expectations. But it's the inconsistency that is maddening.

Again, it is not consistent with the brand promise as displayed on the website or in the advertising. The worst part is that consumers in this category expect this level of poor customer service and the confusing array of billing arrangements. Consumers are not surprised by poor service, so they have relatively low expectations. But it's the inconsistency that is maddening. Verizon directly promises to be the exact opposite. So the brand sets up an expectation that consumers will be satisfied like never before. The resulting inconsistency is even worse than it would have been had the promise never been made.

There is a huge disconnect between the advertising and website touchpoints and the monthly billing, customer service, and retail store touchpoints. The inconsistency is so incredible that it's hard to believe that it's all from the same brand. Particularly when the advertising and website present the brand one way and the other touchpoints present the brand quite another way. So, sure, the wireless coverage is unbeatable, but the rest of the brand experience is frustrating.

Not that the brand should promise confusing billing and poor service, but it should at least be consistent in its marketing across its touchpoints, from advertising to website to retail store to monthly billing statement to customer service representatives.

Entire advocacy groups have formed around sharing the disappointing experiences with Verizon. Check out hateverizon.org and listen to consumers banding together and sharing their bad experiences with Verizon. One blogger even recorded his phone call with several incompetent Verizon customer service representatives over a billing issue. This is a great example of the power of the consumer reacting to a poor experience effect—a wake-up call for marketers.

Now I know that the same can be said of the other brands in the category, like AT&T, T-Mobile, and Sprint. Those brands are just as guilty. Verizon has the opportunity to change the category dynamic and promises to do so. But the brand doesn't deliver on it. As a result, it's hard to say exactly what the brand is all about.

The end result? Chaos, misunderstanding, disappointment, poor business results, just like we described in chapter two. This is why positive consistency is a cornerstone of the experience effect and of the brand's success.

Don't get me wrong, marketers do not set out to create a set of inconsistent experiences. No one wants to do a bad job. Stuff just sometimes gets in the way. On bigger brands at larger companies, I've seen inconsistent brand experiences across touchpoints partly because different teams were executing the work. One team will concentrate on the advertising while another team will bring the online world to life, for example.

Some brands are just so big that it's difficult to monitor all the marketing activity or to understand what the various parts of the brand are promising in the marketplace. That may very well be the case with Verizon, where the company has different teams managing wireless, landline, Internet, and cable services. Because marketing work is so subjective, consistent execution is in the eye of the beholder, and different people may see the exact same strategy differently, which gets played out in the communication touchpoints differently.

One way around this is to have a well-communicated brand definition and a solid consumer understanding via a consumer profile that is shared and embraced across all members of all teams that touch the brand. Execution will still be subjective, but at least we can narrow the gap.

A thorough consumer profile would tell the marketers at Verizon how important customer service is to the consumers and how misled consumers feel by the brand's advertising promises.

Another reason we see inconsistent marketing is that brand managers, in their effort to prioritize the more important touchpoints, do not always put enough effort into every touchpoint. They delegate the less important ones to less senior team members or to lower budget allocations and don't take the time to monitor the work. They make the assumption that because the touchpoint is not as important, it doesn't warrant the effort and won't have a tremendous impact on the market.

For Verizon, it certainly feels like the management team has prioritized advertising touchpoints over customer service touchpoints. In a service business, I would prioritize the touchpoints differently, which would certainly help to differentiate Verizon in a marketplace filled with poor customer service. If the brand is using a touchpoint, then it's a brand priority to some degree, and no touchpoint should be left underdeveloped. To me, customer service should be the number one priority. Even when it's just a follow-up e-mail to the brand's list of consumers, for example, it's still a reflection of the brand. It needs to be consistent with all the brand experiences.

Of course every brand and every organization large and small is different. No matter the situation, it's important to use a few tools and processes that will ensure that the brand develops a consistent marketing experience. We will talk about this a lot more in chapter fifteen. It's our job as marketers to not only choose the touchpoints, but also to make sure they are put to their best use, consistently. Just make sure that it's not too consistently, because that can get the brand into trouble too.

CHAPTER **9**

Avoiding the Cookie Cutter
Creating Unique Touchpoints

NOW THAT WE HAVE identified and activated all the touchpoints that make sense for the consumer and for the brand, it's time to add some content. It's time to give each touchpoint a role in the marketing mix—a unique role each time with each touchpoint, but all with the same brand definition that we built up front in chapter three. But how do we know what to do at each touchpoint?

Figuring this out is what gives the experience effect its true meaning and content, and it's where the brand adds even more value to consumers' lives. Ultimately, our job as marketers is to weave the brand's communication into each touchpoint, to take specific marketing communications and turn them into tailored brand messaging, perfectly fitted to the attributes of that touchpoint. If we do it all with a consistent brand identity, then we will truly have built an experience effect.

Our job as marketers is to weave the brand's communication into each touchpoint.

This clearly can be a lot of work. Entire staffs of marketing professionals are dedicated to mapping out the messaging at each touchpoint. When the brands are large, entire teams are sometimes dedicated to just one touchpoint; that's how complex this little exercise in good marketing can become.

All the hard work turns to magic when the tailored messaging at each touchpoint creates a uniquely ownable brand experience. While consistency is the goal, we do need to avoid a cookie cutter approach. We don't want each touchpoint to be exactly the same each time. Yes, the brand experience should be consistent, but it should also be tailored to the venue. Make the experience fit the touchpoint—that's how the ultimate experience effect is created. There's no value added when each touchpoint is exactly the same.

As we map out what to communicate at each touchpoint, it is important to understand the medium and its role in the consumer's life. What does the consumer need or want at that touchpoint? If the touchpoint is television, for example, then the consumer may want to be entertained or find something new or escape or even channel surf. Depending on the time of day, the consumer may want the latest news and information. It depends on the consumer and the context within their day.

This kind of thinking is applicable to every touchpoint, not just television. If a website is part of the brand experience, for example, then think through why the brand's consumers are online and why they might visit and navigate the brand website. We need to think through how a brand website can help build the right kind of experience for the consumer, unique from the other touchpoints in the marketing plan.

Too many marketers just automatically, almost out of habit, put together a formulaic website to mirror either other elements of the marketing plan or other brands in the company portfolio. This approach does not effectively maximize the website touchpoint for the specific brand and how it can engage the consumer. In this case, the website content and navigation should perfectly reflect what those particular consumers of that particular brand need and want. Those needs and wants might very well differ from those at other touchpoints; the website experience should be different from a printed brochure, for example.

The website's purpose might not necessarily be to distribute brand information; it might be to connect consumers together to share their own personal experiences. Or it might be to offer the latest news in the category, because the website is so easily updated.

The next logical step in the development of the experience effect is to take the touchpoints we have prioritized and try to figure out why consumers are there at that moment, and then maximize each touchpoint individually. We now need to create the experience at the touchpoint, tailoring the brand message there to make it effective. This should be easy, because we know our consumers so well.

Of course there are many important touchpoints within a given marketing plan, as we identified in chapter eight. Packaging is often another one, so, as with a website, think through the value that the packaging should bring to the brand's marketing and tailor the experience to deliver on consumers' needs. To illustrate the point, let's talk this through a bit more.

> *Packaging is so important because it serves many roles in creating the experience effect.*

Packaging is so important because it serves many roles in creating the experience effect, including shelf impact at retail, usage instructions for the consumer, and of course aesthetics, just to name the obvious few. It varies depending on the category. In some categories, like skin care or breakfast cereal, packaging is more crucial to the brand experience than in others, particularly where shelf impact needs to be balanced with aesthetic design or with usage instructions. Skin care and makeup brands place particular importance on the packaging to deliver a vital component of the experience effect in terms of conveying a specific image and making the product easy to apply. If you think about it, it's the packaging that communicates the brand's perceived quality, price, and efficacy in these kinds of cosmetic brands. For cereal, the packaging experience is all about getting noticed on the shelf at retail, and then delivering information or entertainment as the cereal is consumed at home. Think Kellogg's Frosted Flakes with Tony the Tiger on the front panel with nutritional content on the side panel and games for the kids on the back panel.

If the brand is a hand lotion, then perhaps it should have packaging that has a decorative feel so that the consumer keeps it out on the bathroom counter at home. If the brand is a cough medicine, then the packaging will certainly have specific usage instructions but perhaps it should also have other tips for the caregiver of the family, perhaps even a built-in dosage meter to ensure product safety. In these examples, the packaging needs must be balanced with attracting attention on the store shelf. Shelf impact is vitally important to the purchase process for consumer packaged goods.

If the packaging in these cases were just duplicate approaches from the other touchpoints, then it would not be maximized as a touchpoint and the experience effect would be lost. The packaging wouldn't have the level of usage instructions, aesthetic appeal, or shelf impact that it needs to engage consumers. As marketers, we need to think through all these issues thoroughly. In the hand lotion example:

- How do we maximize the packaging so that the consumer has a positive experience using the product?

- How do we balance usage instructions and ingredients with branding?

- How do we deliver a decorative feel while still standing out on the shelf in the store?

The point here is to take each of the touchpoints and outline why they might be important to the consumer, to take the brand messaging and turn it into an experience at that touchpoint, specifically tailored to work for the brand.

When adding a decorative feel to packaging meant to be on display in a consumer's home, make it beautifully consistent with the brand character. Home fragrance companies like Glade attempt to do this with packaging specifically designed for home decor.

Compare the Glade packaging to a more upscale brand like Votivo candles, and we can see two brands in the same general category that have tailored their packaging as a specific touchpoint for their consumers—and for their brand definition. The two brands are sold in very different retail venues. Glade can be found at typical food, drug, and mass merchandiser locations, whereas Votivo is sold only through exclusive boutiques and specialty online retailers. If you notice, the package design for each brand is suited to the retail environment where each brand's consumers shop.

Similarly, when adding usage instructions to cough medicine packaging, present the information in a manner consistent with the brand definition and suited to the needs of the consumers. Think about the range of consumers and all of their needs—there may be cultural and language needs that must be addressed on the packaging in order for the brand to be used properly.

These suggestions and anecdotes are examples of how to think about using the various touchpoints uniquely and how to make sure they fit the brand definition as well as consumer needs and wants.

We need to be insightful and creative. It's all too easy to take a cookie cutter approach to building experiences each time. Don't take the simple route and apply the same messaging in the same format to all the touchpoints—to the advertising, website, and packaging, as we've been discussing. Don't simply reformat the brand experience and reapply the same information each time.

Marketers do this thinking they are doing integrated marketing. It is certainly integrated, but that might not be enough to be effective. Just a few years ago, the term integrated marketing was all the rage. Marketers consciously strove to apply the same messaging to each marketing element in a linear, consistent manner. Not that marketing shouldn't be integrated; of course it should. But that doesn't mean it has to be identical as a result. At the time, integrated thinking was a good step forward and smart marketing. At least it was an improvement over being inconsistent with no thought put toward it, and it was a lot better than each touchpoint creating a completely different experience.

It's still common to see the cookie cutter approach between print brochures and websites, often driven by the package design. These are three touchpoints that really should be developed in uniquely tailored ways. There's a great marketing opportunity to tailor the content to the medium—to create the experience effect.

Many marketers simply take their brochure content and put it online. We hear people describe this approach as brochure-ware—in other words, the content from a printed brochure and a packaging insert are simply uploaded and reformatted onto a website. I would point out that while this may create an integrated approach and may offer great consistency, it does not fully utilize the online touchpoint for what it can bring to the consumer.

Packaging or even a package insert serves a very different purpose from a brochure or a website. A good marketer who understands the experience effect would maximize the consumer experience at each one of those marketing vehicles. Use packaging for what it does best and a website for what it does best. Tailor the touchpoints!

The experience effect takes integrated marketing to the next level by ensuring that the marketing is not only integrated and consistent, but also tailored to each particular touchpoint.

Let's take a look at a real brand to bring the point home. Southwest Airlines does integrated marketing so well because the brand managers use a consistent but tailored approach for their touchpoints. Southwest Airlines is a dynamic example of the experience effect in the marketplace. Coincidence? Not if you believe in the power of good marketing. Southwest Airlines offers an entirely consistent customer experience from touchpoint to touchpoint that is perfectly tailored each time. Southwest is not the only airline that attempts this, but it certainly stands out as one of the best.

The flight attendants' style and personality is a core part of the Southwest brand personality. Log onto YouTube and see some of the flight attendants in action for yourself.

Let's start with the flight attendants. They are incredible brand ambassadors, the best in the business in my view. Unlike on most other airlines, the flight attendants go out of their way to serve their customers and to make them comfortable flying. They are real people with their own style and personality. Each flight attendant brings his or her own unique take to the job, often with a flare of entertainment. The flight attendants' style and personality is a core part of the Southwest brand personality. Log onto YouTube and see some of the flight attendants in action for yourself.

The Southwest website is also chock-full of online tools to help the reservation and flight tracking process, all presented in an organized, logical fashion. Some of the tools can even be downloaded onto a mobile device or to a desktop. As a customer, there are multiple options to make a reservation online, over the phone, or with a mobile device. You can check in at the airport, or ahead of time on a mobile device, or on the website. You can track flight status with these various options as well, including a desktop widget that can be downloaded. The airline offers a range of customer service options for a range of consumers' needs and lifestyles, consistently served up as a core part of the brand experience. Sure, other airlines offer similar services, but none as comprehensive and consistent as Southwest Airlines.

The airline has also avoided many of the trappings of the industry and its resulting financial woes. I can't necessarily comment on the financials of the company, but I do know that Southwest has not penny-pinched its customers for snacks, luggage, or seating like many of the other airlines. There was even a reality television show on A&E that followed the day-to-day lives of Southwest employees: *Airline*. It's still up on YouTube, as a matter of fact. The show highlighted employees dealing with all sorts of customer service issues as effectively as possible. Many were handled in a manner consistent with the brand character, and some were not (I'm sure for the effect of good television). The difference was striking, and certainly not all of marketing can be perfect.

Customer convenience and service does seem to be the priority for Southwest Airlines, as shown on the website and certainly with the flight attendants. These few touchpoints, from the flight attendants to the website to the airline services, all point to a string of consistent experiences surrounding the customer with service. Each touchpoint is uniquely created to deliver the same level of service in a slightly different way for each and every customer.

On the flipside, let's look at an example of consistent marketing that is all too cookie cutter, integrated marketing that is perhaps a bit too integrated.

Pottery Barn. I love Pottery Barn, I really do. Whenever I walk by a retail store or receive a catalog in the mail, I stop and browse. Sometimes I buy, particularly when items are on sale, but not always. I'm a browser at heart at Pottery Barn. There's an episode of *Friends* that has the characters buying some furniture there—hysterical and dead on. Rachel buys a coffee table from Pottery Barn but tells Phoebe that she bought the table at a flea market because Phoebe hates Pottery Barn and thinks that all its furniture is mass produced and exactly the same. Phoebe figures it out though when she visits Ross's apartment to find the exact same coffee table. It is an accurate take on the Pottery Barn experience.

Take a look at the Pottery Barn catalog, website, and retail stores, however, and notice that not only are these touchpoints completely consistent, they are all completely identical! Store to store, store to catalog, and catalog to website. Furniture item to furniture item, as depicted in the *Friends* episode. Consistency is good, don't get me wrong. No matter which retail store you walk into, the brand experience is the same. Products and sales support is identical store to store. Catalogs and website too. They are all good experiences, but what I find interesting is that these experiences are not at all tailored for the medium.

These three touchpoints are almost too consistent; they are not unique to the specific venue. Nicely done, but not tailored for the particular set of consumers who may prefer one medium over the other. The marketing is still good, but I believe that Pottery Barn is missing the opportunity to make each touchpoint even more engaging for its consumers.

To a great extent, there are different types of consumers who shop at retail stores as compared to catalogs or websites. Consumers choose shopping outlets based on their own personal browsing and purchasing needs and wants. Even an individual consumer is looking at the venues to do different things. The retail store might bring the products to life in a more real-world environment, while the catalog aids in browsing. The website might help comparison shop and ultimately close the deal. It's important to know which consumers are at each touchpoint and why they are there—and to tailor the experience as a result.

A more specialized experience effect for Pottery Barn could include tailored experiences at each of the touchpoints to more completely fulfill consumer needs and wants at that point. Tailoring the touchpoints helps to make sure that the brand experience is at its best, all along the way. Tailoring touchpoints would help Pottery Barn build more in-depth experiences for its various kinds of consumers and their shopping behaviors. It might even promote more frequent browsing and purchasing. Perhaps the catalogs could feature articles from the Pottery Barn designers on how to accessorize a room. The website could offer a sorting feature for easy item and price comparison.

I find looking at these kinds of examples to be so helpful in turning a theoretical concept, like avoiding the cookie cutter approach, into a real-world learning opportunity. We can learn from each other when we observe each other's work. It can also be very inspiring, particularly when we observe some of the greats in the industry.

CHAPTER **10**

Meet Martha, Louis, and Some Elves
Finding Inspiration

AS THEY SAY, success is part inspiration, part perspiration. Let's look at exemplary parts of the experience effect that some would consider to be the best of a touchpoint at work. By examining a few great works of marketing, you will personally become inspired to do your own.

Martha Stewart. Talk about some controversy, right? You either love her or hate her; there are not a lot of folks in between. Forget about the celebrity portion for a minute and consider a brand that I believe demands a great deal of respect. Take a look at two of the brand's touchpoints within the experience effect: *Martha Stewart Living* and Stewart's show, *The Martha Stewart Show*. In reality, these are both touchpoints and products, and they both ladder up to the Martha Stewart brand.

Regardless of your affinity for Martha Stewart the person, you have to admit that the Martha Stewart brand has been marketed quite well. The magazine is the perfect embodiment of the brand, perfectly executed in its format. The show does the same, except that it is expertly executed in a daytime television show format, much like her daytime cable television show from more than a few years back. I'm not talking about the content per se, or about Martha Stewart the celebrity (although we will discuss celebrities in more detail in chapter eleven). I'm simply referring to the Martha Stewart brand experience between two specific touchpoints.

The magazine and television show are each executed to the medium's best use. They are exact representations of the brand and they work in tandem with each other. But they are not identical. *The Martha Stewart Show* features a daily celebrity guest, which plays well to a daytime talk show viewing audience. *Martha Stewart Living* follows a different yet still consistent format, as it focuses more on the details of completing a home project, be it cooking, crafting, organizing, or gardening—especially if it's the classic Thanksgiving dinner as only Martha Stewart can create!

> *It's obvious that Martha Stewart the person has a very good sense of Martha Stewart the brand.*

Both touchpoints also drive consumers to other touchpoints of the brand, including the various brand websites and products available at multiple retail locations. It's obvious that Martha Stewart the person has a very good sense of Martha Stewart the brand. As a consummate brand manager, she knows who her consumers are and what they want, both rationally and emotionally.

I had the unbelievable pleasure of visiting her home in Maine. Talk about an experience! Aside from the splendor of it all, the striking thing about her home is that it's also completely consistent with the Martha Stewart brand. Each room is like a set for the magazine and television show—and in many cases the rooms are used as sets. Her home life, activities, and projects become content for her brand.

Now, obviously, like any brand, Martha Stewart has stumbled. Every brand makes mistakes. It's a part of marketing and of brand evolution. The prime-time television show, which was a spin-off of *The Apprentice,* didn't do anything to build her brand equity or win over new consumers. I'm not sure that it did much for her current consumers either. But the Martha Stewart brand gave it a go and then moved on—nothing wrong with that at all. It's not that the prime-time show was completely inconsistent with the brand; it actually made a lot of sense on some levels. But it may have been too "business" for the brand's core audience. It is a good example of how it's acceptable to experiment with a brand—it's not the end of the world if something fails. If it's a reasonable try, it probably won't hurt the brand equity or positioning with consumers. I don't think it hurt Martha Stewart all that much.

I admire Martha Stewart, not because I love Martha herself or because I am a part of her target market, but because of the way she has created a powerful experience effect between her magazine and her television show (not to mention the other touchpoints and properties).

Let's look at another brand: Louis Vuitton.

Whether you're a *fashionista* or not, you must know Louis Vuitton as a powerful contemporary brand with a rich design heritage. I'm not talking about the product designs, although they are an ideal example of a continually evolving, classic brand. And I'm also not talking about the price points or the clientele, because that starts to get crazy. I am referring to the experience from store to store.

Walking into a Louis Vuitton store is to experience the essence of the brand. The stores offer a mixture of warmth and glamour, of service and exclusivity, and of the obtainable and inaccessible. Each store is uniquely Louis Vuitton, whether on Fifth Avenue in New York, the Bal Harbour Mall in Miami, or the luxurious Wynn Las Vegas Hotel. Same feeling, same branding, same incredible service.

None of the stores ever feels crowded. All of the stores are expertly designed and have just the right amount of merchandise on display, placed around the store in just the right kind of way. Not overpacked but not too sparse either. Just when you think you've seen everything, there's another small display to explore for a few minutes. No two stores are completely alike. The merchandising fits the architecture of the individual store, the specific building, and the neighborhood.

The sales associates seem to be native to the location. While some of the same core items are displayed at each store, the balance of the merchandise is just a little different from location to location to best reflect the consumers who go to that store or to best fit the dynamic attributes of that store's location. So there's a slightly different selection of shoes at the store in Miami from at the New York stores, for example. I've even noticed a more trendy selection of accessories in the SoHo New York store tucked amid art galleries than in the Fifth Avenue New York store located near the big-name fashion boutiques. And these two stores are only a few miles apart!

This is the experience effect at work, store to store, making sure all the retail touchpoints are working their hardest for consumers, giving them the kind of brand experience those specific consumers are looking for at that specific location. It seems like a conscious plan by the Louis Vuitton marketers, and I'm sure they realize that many of their consumers frequent multiple stores. The Fifth Avenue New York store is perfect for the classics during the holidays, the Miami store features the best resort wear, the SoHo store is a sure bet for trendier items, and the Wynn Las Vegas store is well suited for indulgent purchases.

Louis Vuitton is a great example of defining the brand, knowing the consumer, and using retail touchpoints to their best advantage.

Next up—Ralph Lauren.

I do have to call out Ralph Lauren as well for incredible marketing from store to mobile device. Really cool stuff, using great technology—the first in the luxury fashion business. If you've been to any of the Ralph Lauren stores, whether it's Ralph Lauren Classics, Ralph Lauren Rugby, Ralph Lauren Double RL, or any of the brand's properties, then you know that, like Louis Vuitton, they are merchandised wonderfully. Ralph Lauren is merchandised very differently from Louis Vuitton, obviously, because they are fulfilling different consumer needs, rationally and emotionally. Unlike Louis Vuitton, the Ralph Lauren stores are jammed with merchandise. It's a bit of a treasure hunt to get through it all. But it's not a flea market either because the clothes are still beautifully merchandised so that the shopper can easily discover every piece of clothing. Where Louis Vuitton is clean and perfect, Ralph Lauren is deliciously cluttered and packed. Both are eye candy at their finest, but in very different ways.

The stores are beautiful, but the storefront windows are a spectacle. They are fashion stories told visually. The window designers for all the Ralph Lauren stores take the best of the best clothing from the current season's line and miraculously pack it all together in a fascinating story. At Ralph Lauren Rugby in the fall, for example, the windows feature a Halloween theme by showcasing all the merchandise that contain skulls of one form or anoth-

> *These windows serve as incredible brand ambassadors, even when a store is closed.*

er. The windows have a frenetic yet extravagant "frightening" feel to them. These windows serve as incredible brand ambassadors, even when a store is closed. In fact, at night the windows are even more spectacular as the lighting is so perfectly woven around the clothing. You can see everything clearly, even from across the street. It's common to see people glancing longingly into the windows when the stores are closed, often for several minutes at a time.

Here's where the experience effect perfection lies. From store to store, the brand is certainly maximizing a unique experience in the storefront windows. But the kicker is that the storefront windows actually give consumers the opportunity to shop, even when the store is closed. On select windows at certain stores there is a bar code that can be captured with a mobile device that then links to the Ralph Lauren website. So when a consumer sees an item in the window and wants to buy it, the mobile device allows for an instant connection and a seamless merchandise selection. This is not digital marketing for digital marketing's sake. This is a well-thought-out branding experience that is completely consistent with not only the purpose of the storefront windows, but also the Ralph Lauren brand and the shopping behavior of the Ralph Lauren consumer.

It wouldn't work for every fashion brand, but it certainly works for Ralph Lauren. Interestingly, the brand does not use this technology at every single store. It uses it in those store locations in certain markets such as New York City and Miami's South Beach, where there is a consumer base that will appreciate it and use it. The brand is even starting to use these codes in some of its print advertising.

Mobile technology that allows a consumer to shop directly online from the storefront window (or print ad). Brilliant.

Let's step out of the fashion world and into the grocery store with Keebler cookies and crackers.

A great example of using two touchpoints, the package and the website, is the Keebler brand and its magical little elves. The Keebler elves and their home in the Hollow Tree have become branded legends, representing the brand equity of a beloved line of cookies and crackers. As a core part of the brand equity, they are prominently featured on every package and are central to experiencing the brand, both at retail and at home. Log onto the website and a Keebler elf shows the way into the hollow tree. The website literally takes the packaging and brings it to life. It is completely engaging and a wonderful experience, especially if you are a lover of Keebler cookies and crackers. But it is not overdone either, because quite honestly that would be out of brand character. It's filled with great little recipes and promotions to help save money, all compiled to satisfy the needs of its target consumers, rationally and emotionally.

It is truly an inspiring experience, from packaging to website, and sometimes retail displays too. At certain times of the year— like the holiday season, back to school, or during the summer—the hollow tree comes to life at the end of grocery store aisles. The retail displays feature a three-dimensional version of the hollow tree where the Keebler elves display the cookies and crackers. With that display, the products are easy to put into the shopping cart, always at a featured low price. The kids love it, which I'm sure is exactly the point. A consistent brand experience yet again.

We've been talking about some of the usual suspects when it comes to touchpoints, both traditional forms like packaging and some of the newer forms like mobile devices. But as we discussed in chapter seven, touchpoints can come in many forms, depending on the consumer profile and the brand definition. Live contact with a representative of the company can be such an incredibly important part of the experience effect. It should be a consistent part of the brand experience just like any other touchpoint, like Southwest Airlines.

American Express understands the importance of live contact as part of its brand experience. Whenever I call the customer service line at American Express, after a quick menu of options, I am generally greeted by a live customer service representative with the utmost of professionalism. I have personally had to contact American Express customer service many times through the years, and every single time I have had my issue resolved consistently and efficiently.

For me, the live customer service at American Express absolutely lives up to how the brand presents itself in its other touchpoints, like television and print advertising.

I'm sure you can personally relate. How many times have you called a company for customer service and been met by an automated voice that walks you through one list of options after another, only to be sent through an endless loop of numbered options? And when you finally do get a live person, he or she is sometimes unbelievably hard to understand and often does not have the authority or knowledge to help.

Disgruntled consumers who consistently cannot find help from a live customer service representative have created entire websites and blogs to band together. In the age of user-generated content and up-to-the-minute status updates, poor customer service can quickly destroy a brand's equity. If personal service is part of how the brand is defined, then it needs to be woven into the most relevant touchpoints for the brand, including the employees and how they handle customer service individually and as a group, and particularly those employees who interact with consumers. Receptionists, greeters, client service managers, all are a part of the experience effect.

In the age of user-generated content and up-to-the-minute status updates, poor customer service can quickly destroy a brand's equity.

How about you and your brand? If customer service is important to your brand's success, make sure it is a consistent part of the experience effect, just like for American Express. Use this brand as inspiration to build proper customer service into the brand's experience, across as many touchpoints as makes sense. Also use the other great marketers highlighted in this chapter to inspire breakthrough interactions throughout the entire marketing plan, including advertising, website, online, retail, and packaging—as well as all the others.

Feeling inspired? Now let's take the brand experience to the extreme—to the red carpet.

CHAPTER **11**

Madonna and Tide
Learning from Celebrities

EVERY BRAND CAN LEARN from the success of the masters and from the marketing choices they have made. In many ways, creating a marketing plan is all about making the proper choices that will build the business. I thought it would be insightful and fun to take a look at a different kind of marketing—brands that are constantly making choices to build their business.

Celebrities have a product to sell, so why shouldn't we think of them as brands too? As brand marketers, we have to choose our brand definition, choose the target market, and choose the touchpoints that make the most sense. So do celebrities. Every day we make choices as marketers. Celebrities are no different—they make critical choices every day too:

- Who else makes more high-profile choices than a celebrity?

- Who else's product lives or dies by the marketing and publicity that gets generated?

- Who else has their personal choices paraded across marketing vehicles, good, bad, or indifferent?

Their career success is a direct result of the choices that they make, much like a marketer's success with a brand. Consumer perceptions of their celebrity brand are influenced by every movie role they select, every public appearance they make, and every dress they wear.

If celebrities thought of themselves as brands, more of them would have greater career longevity.

If celebrities thought of themselves as brands, I would wager that more of them would have greater career longevity. If celebrities thought about their own experience effect, they would make more consistent choices to build their brand experience.

Don't get me wrong. I know that many celebrities consider themselves to be artists and not marketers, and I respect them for it. No one is more of a celebrity lover then I am; it's a hobby that I participate in constantly. I am a voracious consumer of all things entertainment, and I love pop culture. So I have tremendous respect for celebrity talent, artistry, lifestyle, and all the hard work that goes into it, just like I have tremendous respect for what brands can offer.

Artists sing, act, write, dance, and paint—and when they aspire and grow to commercial success, they often become celebrities, some with big production machines behind them and others on a smaller, more local scale. In either case, with some level of commercial success comes the need to do some marketing. So these artists begin to make appearances, they build websites, and many participate in social media.

They start to have a brand personality, consciously or not, and they promote it. Heck, they even have packaging when you get right down to it. Look at the alignments that the bigger celebrities have with fashion designers for their clothing and accessories. They may not call it a marketing partnership, but that is certainly what it is. The notion of celebrity has greatly expanded in our culture beyond just the artistry that I mentioned. Talent is no longer a strict requirement, and in fact good marketing can be a perfect substitute. Look at the proliferation of reality television shows and the lengths that the "stars" go to in order to stay famous.

Celebrities are brands that need to be marketed. If they only thought about it that way, they'd probably be better brands and more consistently commercially successful as a result. Every time a new movie, album, or television show is released, a marketing machine kicks into gear to promote it, with the celebrity at the front and center.

It's no coincidence that before every major movie release, the featured celebrity is suddenly on the cover of every magazine and appearing on every talk show. Or suddenly there's a major controversy surrounding that celebrity that explodes his or her name and face across the tabloids—all over tmz.com and perezhilton.com. The same is true of television shows, Broadway musicals, concert tours, and the like. Have you seen the machine for *American Idol* kick in just as the new season is approaching? Just a coincidence? Hardly—it's no different from a touchpoint map if you ask me. Good marketing is no coincidence.

In some cases, the celebrity is the talent, like with an album from any favorite singer or musician. In other cases, the celebrity is the hook for the marketing, like with a movie. In some cases, the celebrity is both the talent and the hook. But in all cases, just like with Keebler or Louis Vuitton, the brand is producing something for consumers to consume, even if it's just a moment of live entertainment or a music download.

A movie with a talented big-ticket celebrity like George Clooney increases the likelihood of success for the film. George Clooney becomes the marketing vehicle for the movie, along with an intense media plan across touchpoints. In this case, George Clooney becomes the hook, or the draw, because he already has a fan base (or a consumer target market).

In some cases, the celebrity is merely a celebrity with all that celebrity represents. Many celebrities get appearance fees just to show up to clubs, particularly new clubs trying to get on the nightlife circuit, or classic ones trying to stay hot. In this case, the celebrity is also a marketing hook, and can be an engaging one at that.

Paris Hilton has made a career out of being a celebrity, and she is often paid to leverage her brand to just show up. Paris Hilton can drive traffic to a new club, for example, which is no different from a paid media insertion or touchpoint. Buying a brand ad in *People* magazine is really no different from paying Paris Hilton to show up at your club. In both cases, a brand is spending money to drive awareness and to generate sales.

No matter how you slice it, celebrities are brands. When you hear about the $20–million plus salary that Brad Pitt gets for a movie, it's easy to forget that Brad Pitt is actually a company. He has staff to pay that includes lawyers, promoters, assistants, and agents. The salary goes to the Brad Pitt company to cover the costs of the Brad Pitt brand. That might not be how he looks at it or how most celebrities look at it, but as a marketer I don't really see the difference. Brad Pitt is a brand with a specific brand experience that people have come to expect in the career choices he makes. Fans are more than willing to pay to see the actor they respect portray quirky characters, and they love to see the man they respect do great works of charity, even if he's not so friendly in public or even in interviews. It's all part of his elusive brand personality.

Marketing is marketing, regardless of the brand or category—celebrities are brands too. Does that make a celebrity any different from Gillette? Depends on how talented they are and how well they are marketed. I may be the first to compare a celebrity like Julia Roberts to a Gillette Mach 3 Turbo shaver, but I think it's a fair comparison. Gillette has to keep reinventing itself, coming up with new products to stay current. Julia Roberts has to keep reinventing herself, taking on new roles to stay current. On both accounts, those are brands.

> *I may be the first to compare a celebrity like Julia Roberts to a Gillette Mach 3 Turbo shaver, but I think it's a fair comparison.*

I'm talking way beyond the new celebrity fragrance sold at department stores. Way more than Britney Spears Curious at a Macy's counter. I'm talking Madonna territory.

I'm not the first to say that Madonna is a brilliant marketer, but I'll take it one step further and say that Madonna is a quintessential brand. Madonna is perhaps the epitome of celebrity marketing and celebrity branding. Right from the very beginning of her career, she was a bit of a bad girl. Well, maybe more than a bit. Even as she has so famously reinvented herself through the years, she has always been a bit of a bad girl. That's how she has defined her brand. Even as a mother, her brand is still bad girl. I'm sure she's a great mom, but if you notice, her bad girl image has stayed intact. She even had an unconventional arrangement with her first child, very much in keeping with her personality and brand. And as she has gone through her divorces, no one has held that against her, neither the divorce itself nor the circumstances surrounding it. It's just Madonna being Madonna.

It's also no coincidence that many of Madonna's escapades have coincided with the release of one of her products. With each release of a new album or music video, the Madonna brand has been in full force, knowing the brand definition well and being executed with an exquisite use of touchpoints.

As a marketer taking a look at Madonna's amazingly long career in the entertainment business, I can see that her constant reinvention is not revolutionary thinking for a brand. It might be for a celebrity, but not for a brand. Madonna's constant reinvention is really just a continual evolution of a brand, a brand that knows what it is and knows its consumers. The brand must evolve to stay current in the marketplace and with the needs of its consumers, rationally and emotionally. Madonna has certainly created her own brand experience. She's not the only one to do this for sure—take a look at Rod Stewart or David Bowie. But her ability to weave herself into pop culture, continually over time, is what stands Madonna apart. And just when it appears that the Madonna brand has run its course, she releases a new album of classic Madonna and her fans are celebrating again (and watching her be a bit of a bad girl on video).

In many ways, the Madonna brand of entertainment is no different from Tide laundry detergent.

In many ways, the Madonna brand of entertainment is no different from Tide laundry detergent. Both Madonna and Tide know exactly who they are as a brand, and both have had a consistent identity for decades. The brands have evolved through the years while still staying close to their equity. Both have had new competitors come and go, often at great risk to their brands, and both have shown great staying power. Madonna's continual reinvention is similar to Tide introducing variations of laundry detergent each year to keep up with ever-changing consumer needs, like high-efficiency detergent for the new washers, and like a new album filled with the latest tech-no-dance music. Or color-safe bleach for new fabrics and colors, or a book about erotica to coincide with music of the same name and genre. But it's always laundry detergent that gets the family clothes clean, so that they can all put their best face forward. And it's always pop entertainment from a bit of a bad girl.

While Madonna has evolved through the years as a brand, her brand personality and essence have remained true to her core. In her own words, she creates good pop music, nothing more, nothing less. She drives pop culture and is a fashion icon; she knows it and she uses it. That has been consistent with every part of the Madonna experience effect. She has a very true sense of herself, and I believe that she views her celebrity as a brand. Maybe not a brand like Tide, but a brand nonetheless.

Her public appearances and every part of her experience effect are entirely consistent. One of her concert tours was called "Sticky and Sweet" to support her *Hard Candy* album, and she has released highly controversial books and DVDs through the years. Take a look at her website, and it is all things Madonna, including her entire portfolio of music videos, like any good brand. No inconsistency here. It should be no surprise that Madonna is not a critically acclaimed actress or that her film career has been so erratic. I don't really think it's even about her talent as an actress, although I know there are people who would disagree. It's not really in her brand definition to be a serious actress. No one needs or wants her to be a serious actress. Even her appearances on talk shows are consistent with her brand. Madonna is not suddenly a different person when talking to David Letterman. Quite the contrary, she is consistently a combination of funny, seductive, and foul-mouthed—all a part of the Madonna brand experience effect.

She was critically acclaimed in *Evita,* but that makes sense because the movie was a musical about a bit of a bad girl. It was a perfect connection and her consumers embraced it. It was also marketed brilliantly to her fan base, including tie-ins to fashion and makeup as well as music remixes for the clubs. Amazingly tailored touchpoints, or what?!

Although she has tried to be a serious actress and failed somewhat, her consumer audience does not fault her; they almost expect it because it's in keeping with their sense of her brand. As I have mentioned, every brand stumbles and makes mistakes. It's perfectly acceptable to experiment, as long as in the long run the brand sticks to its essence.

Madonna is the epitome of a celebrity brand, and hence she has had incredible career longevity, particularly when compared to others in her field. Her experience effect has been tremendously successful over the long term. It is far more typical, as a celebrity, to have only a window of time in the spotlight. I would maintain as a brand marketer that there is a reason for that.

If celebrities were to think of themselves as brands and were to utilize the concept of the experience effect, they would have a clear brand definition of who they are, like Madonna and like Tide have. They would truly understand the wants and needs of their fan base, their consumers, like Madonna and Tide do. And they would make sure they built a brand or celebrity experience consistently across every touchpoint.

Many celebrities stumble when it comes to this because they don't think of themselves necessarily as brands, they don't tend to worry about being consistent. They jump from genre to genre in their pursuit of creativity or of fame, and then consumers don't really know who they really are. They make bad choices, as people and as brands. Look at Jennifer Love Hewitt and her failed attempts at various genres, from television shows to movies to albums. I bet most people don't know the Jennifer Love Hewitt brand of entertainment because it is so undefined.

Witness Jessica Simpson versus Madonna. Can anyone really say who Jessica Simpson is as a celebrity or even as an artist? She has moved around musical genres and at the same time has tried to be a serious actress. She has tried to be the normal everyday wife with naiveté and sincerity, and yet she has been embroiled in tabloid controversy. Jessica Simpson, compared to Madonna, had a small window of success that she has been struggling to climb back into ever since. Madonna has been in her own window all along, despite weathering many similar personal storms.

Madonna is a brand; Jessica Simpson is someone who was famous for seemingly a few minutes. Arguably, they both have their own unique talents, but the difference is their use of the experience effect.

Of course, celebrities are not the only brands who have a limited window of success unless they are well marketed. You could almost parallel the career of Jessica Simpson with the brands Von Dutch or FUBU. Hot for a very short time, and then struggling to be noticed for the remainder. Without really understanding what they are as a brand, they jump on a particular trend and ride it until it runs out of fashion.

Just a short time ago, we couldn't turn a page in a magazine without seeing the Von Dutch logo somewhere, as with Jessica Simpson. But because Von Dutch didn't really know what it was as a brand and didn't really develop a good understanding of its consumer base, it faded away almost as quickly as it became hot. Von Dutch didn't define itself as a brand, and it made bad choices by expanding quickly into boutique stores that were not at all unique and that were also loaded with merchandise no one wanted. Sure the T-shirts and hats were popular for a fashion minute, but the brand buzz quickly faded. Too bad Von Dutch didn't define its brand to the same extent Madonna does—perhaps it could have built a unique branded retail experience and been more successful.

I'll take this analogy even further to say that celebrity brands are a lot like pharmaceutical brands. Both have a long development process, and only a few brands finally make it to a big launch. There are no overnight successes in either industry and a lot of brands end up on the cutting room floor. Then the few that make it big have a window of incredible hype and success, with some controversy thrown in. Then someone else comes along with a bigger claim to fame and takes its place. Witness Shania Twain and Singulair. Along came Carrie Underwood and Nasonex.

Madonna is not the only brand in the entertainment business. We can learn from several celebrity brands. Take a look at Lady Gaga, a new entertainment brand right on the heels of Madonna. The music, costumes, performances, appearances, and marketing partnerships all add up to an incredible experience effect that I am predicting will have career longevity. Lady Gaga gets it—her brand is all about creativity and self-expression. Hence her work with Polaroid as creative director for a new line of products works seamlessly with her music. She is a brand well on her way to superstar status, which will force Madonna to step it up once again.

And then there is Dolly Parton—you know what that brand is all about. It is homespun music, movies, television shows, theme parks, even a Broadway show—lots of touchpoints that are all uniquely Dolly Parton, growing and evolving through the years as her consumers grow and evolve too. Regardless of the touchpoint, it's only Dolly Parton and no one else. Dolly's old friend Kenny Rogers tried to launch a chain of fast-food restaurants. It made no sense for his brand and the restaurants failed.

If marketing is all about choices, then the brand Sean "P. Diddy" Combs has made some really smart choices.

Jon Stewart is well on his way to being a great brand. He brings his unique comedy and political satire to a wide variety of touchpoints from his own cable television show to books and guest appearances. If he plays his career like a brand with an experience effect, then I'm predicting a big consumer base and career longevity.

Sean "P. Diddy" Combs is another example. He turned his energy toward writing, producing, rapping, and even acting into more than just an entertainment brand: a lifestyle brand. Music, entertainment, fashion, attitude—lifestyle. If you are in his consumer target, you can live the Sean "P. Diddy" Combs life. If marketing is all about choices, then the brand Sean "P. Diddy" Combs has made some really smart choices, much like Martha Stewart, Louis Vuitton, Ralph Lauren, and Keebler have.

One last point here: Marketing is marketing, regardless of the category. It doesn't matter if the brand is a pop music superstar or laundry detergent. The basic principles of good marketing remain the same:

- Know who you are as a brand.

- Understand your consumer.

- Build a consumer experience.

- Create that experience consistently and uniquely across all touchpoints.

- Continually evolve and grow.

- Make good choices.

- Learn from examples in the marketplace.

- Reap the business rewards.

In other words, create an experience effect—celebrity or consumer packaged good. But all of us, famous or otherwise, could use a little research to prove our marketing worth.

CHAPTER 12

Everyone Else Bring Data
Researching the Experience Effect

WE TALKED IN CHAPTERS four and five about understanding the consumer and about how to do grassroots-type research to get a deeper sense of the consumer's life. In this chapter we are not delving into research to understand the consumer, but instead we are going to explore research on the actual brand experience we've been creating. We will do research to test the marketing work we've done.

Research to understand consumers is often done at the beginning, although admittedly it should really be done throughout the entire process. Experience effect research, on the other hand, is done toward the end of the process, although it should also be done throughout. Specific touchpoint research like observing website navigation or measuring print advertising recall at the end of the process can give us the proof we need that the brand experience we've created will perform well in the marketplace. Research on the touchpoints you're working on can help make sure the marketing will connect with consumers. Of course we don't have to wait until the very end, because we can test our work while we are developing it.

All along in the process, we've been using our judgment in selecting touchpoints and tailoring our messaging for them. Research can now make sure that our judgment is correct. It can prove that we are right, and it can help us avoid making a mistake twice. And it can certainly shed light on something we may not have otherwise known.

> *"In God We Trust, Everyone Else Bring Data."*

There was a very talented company president who was my client years ago who had a huge sign over his door that said, "In God We Trust, Everyone Else Bring Data." The sign made me laugh every time I walked by. Most people never heard him say, "Use your judgment." He believed that every decision should be backed up by data obtained from good old-fashioned research. If I were to ask him about his philosophy as it relates to the experience effect, he would probably tell me to bring data for each touchpoint to prove that the communication is working at every step. I'm not referring to consumer profiling, but research on the specific touchpoint and how it is being used to build the brand experience.

It is true that research will help define the brand and understand the target consumers up front, but we also need to do research on the experience effect we are building and the experiences we are creating at each touchpoint. This research will then of course also help us to continually grow our understanding of the consumer and the definition of the brand. The various forms of research work hand in hand throughout the process. So in order to make sure we are using good judgment, we'll do some research to back up our thinking. We will ask ourselves some questions, like:

- What should the brand accomplish with the consumer at this touchpoint?

- Are consumers responding to the brand at this touchpoint in the way we had planned?

- Is the brand experience at this touchpoint what the consumer wants and needs?

- Is the brand experience at this touchpoint consistent with the other touchpoints?

- Is our brand more effective at this touchpoint than our competition's?

Research will help answer these questions and guide further refinement of the experience effect. In researching brand experiences, start with the easy stuff. Do some relatively easy third-party research that is already available in the public domain. A lot of information doesn't cost anything except for the time it takes to do some digging. These resources will give an idea of what happens at each touchpoint and how to build the experience there.

Take a look at the core competitors and analyze the brand experience they have built at the same touchpoints planned for your brand. You will want to learn from what competitors have done well and also from what they have not done so well. Looking at the competition is the simplest and easiest form of research. It's such a basic foundation because it's sitting right there in plain sight, so take advantage of the research that others have already done. It's the bare minimum, and it's relatively easy to do. We can learn a lot from work that is already in the marketplace. Besides, innovative marketing in one category or industry can certainly be applied to another.

When looking at the competition, think broadly. Many marketers just look at their direct competition to track marketing programs and to stay abreast of what is happening in the category. For example, brands in the candy bar business often track only other competitive candy bar brands. They analyze every move their direct competitors make, examine every piece of communication they put into the marketplace, and track how successful their competitors' marketing programs are in driving sales. They look at every direct competitive use of a touchpoint, but truthfully this is not quite enough. Most marketers are missing a big piece when they limit their tracking. When looking only at direct competitors we miss how the consumer views the category in the context of his or her whole life, and therefore we miss a large part of the real competitive landscape. We need to also look at indirect competitors. This is particularly important when conducting brand experience research, because consumer behavior at any given touchpoint is where all the action happens. It's where the brand is living and where the perceptions are made, and it's also where indirect competition can have its biggest impact on the brand.

Let's continue with candy bars as an example. Consumers who are looking to purchase a candy bar are about to spend a buck or two for a quick indulgence, and it's frequently an impulse purchase. At the point of purchase consumers have a bunch of options in front of them when looking at the candy bar display:

- Snickers or Kit Kat?

- Sweet and creamy or salty and crunchy?

- Bite size and refreshing or large and fulfilling?

- Pure chocolate or mixed with other ingredients?

There are tons of options, right at that moment, for the consumer to choose from. But in reality, candy bar brands are actually competing against many other things at that touchpoint. The consumer is ready to purchase and there are many choices besides other candy bars that could capture that consumer's attention:

- Candy bar or pretzels or chips?

- Candy bar or soft drink?

- Candy bar or ChapStick?

- Candy bar or magazine or newspaper, especially if there's an engaging cover story?

- Waiting in line or rushing back to the office to check e-mail before the next meeting?

At that touchpoint, the candy bar brands are competing against all the things that could get in the way of closing the sale. Some are the direct competitors and some are much more indirect.

So if that touchpoint is a part of the experience effect, it's important to see what consumers are thinking and what all competitors are doing at that moment. Find out what is competing against the brand at every touchpoint. Use competitive intelligence to add some light in a broad sense, and use your judgment. In addition to looking at the entire range of competition, there are other kinds of third-party research, often requiring no monetary investment, that can help in understanding the dynamics of a touchpoint.

Surf the Web to read about associations formed around the touchpoint, such as third-party surveys and seminars, such as eMarketer for Internet touchpoints or POPAI (Point of Purchase Advertising Institute) for retail touchpoints. Business analysts write periodic industry overviews for investors that are readily accessible and informative. Read trade publications to find out what's developing at key touchpoints, particularly in the paid media touchpoints that get a lot of editorial coverage. *Advertising Age* or *AdWeek* are great examples.

Also do some of the more creative, detective-like techniques like reading magazines and surfing websites of interest to the consumer. This time your goal is not just to understand the consumer but also to understand how the consumer interacts with the touchpoint, such as how a consumer navigates a website or responds to an online banner display ad or reads a magazine (which, interestingly, can vary depending on the type of magazine). Firsthand knowledge of how a touchpoint works will help tremendously in analyzing the effectiveness of that touchpoint for making it part of the brand experience.

But stay focused. Too much research and too much data can sometimes hamper good judgment. People call it data overload or analysis paralysis. Stay focused on what you are trying to learn so you can get something out of all your hard work. Use the data to either help shape a decision or help confirm that the right choice was made. Look for data and do research on the specific issue and touchpoint to be maximized. Leave all other data to the side for use on another issue. Stay focused on the question being asked so that the answer is found. We want the research, in this case, to be all about helping to guide what we want the brand experience to be, beyond just brand definition and consumer profiles, and what we want the marketing to accomplish at each touchpoint.

Depending on the research budget, try to get data on each of the touchpoints in the brand experience. Data that will help get the most out of the consumer interaction at that moment in time, specific to the brand. I would suggest literally listing the touchpoints and identifying a research plan for each one. List the touchpoints in priority order of most impact to the business and of most importance to the consumer. Then do a needs assessment for researching the touchpoint and list the research already on hand as well as research needed to both understand the touchpoint and prove that the experience effect is working.

See figure 12.1 for an example of a needs assessment.

This kind of quick needs assessment is invaluable because it will help keep focus and help prioritize the research budget. The needs assessment will help identify areas of currently available data, data from third parties, and where more proprietary research is needed. If I were to apply this kind of needs assessment to our furniture example in chapter five, where we wrote fictional consumer profiles, it might look something like figure 12.2.

Note that the needs assessment clearly outlines where we as the brand managers need to do more research. And it helps to point us in the right direction and keep us focused. The needs assessment will keep us from getting overwhelmed and will help prevent analysis paralysis. It is likely to point out where we need to start doing some of our own proprietary research. Depending on the research budget, we'll want to put some effort into exposing our specific marketing ideas and ele-

> *The needs assessment will keep us from getting overwhelmed and will help prevent analysis paralysis.*

FIGURE 12.1 Research Needs Assessement

Touchpoint	Research Completed	Research Needed to Understand	Research Needed to Prove
Touchpoint 1			
Touchpoint 2			
Touchpoint 3			
Touchpoint 4			
Touchpoint 5			
Touchpoint 6			

ments of the experience effect to consumers to see how they respond. Start with the most critical ones, but don't stop there.

Advertising agencies for years have tried various research methodologies to test the success of television advertising against a specific goal. The methodologies tend to begin with qualitative focus groups responding to storyboards and then build to more quantitative techniques where consumers respond to rough video animatics that depict what the advertising will eventually look

FIGURE 12.2   Furniture Brand Research Needs Assessment

Touchpoint	Research Completed	Research Needed to Understand	Research Needed to Prove
Print Advertising	Data supplied by publications; qualitative focus groups		Quantitative testing
Website	Preliminary qualitative research to observe consumer navigation	Competitive survey of other websites in the category	Monitor website traffic
Catalog	None	Competitive survey of other catalogs in the category	Sales tracking
Online Banner Advertising	Data supplied by websites		Click-through rates
Home Shows	Data supplied by suppliers	Visits to home shows to survey current exhibitors	Traffic studies and need to follow up with home show visitors
Online Couponing Vehicles	Data supplied by websites		Track redemption rates

like. Data comes back to the marketer with key measures on how consumers reacted to the advertising. But this is just one touchpoint among many, and it's not the only one where we can do proprietary research. It is certainly not the only one where we need research to prove out the work that we've done. A common trap that marketers fall into is only conducting research on the more high-profile touchpoints, like television advertising. They will research it to death but then leave the other touchpoints up to chance. They spend all their resources on just a couple of their touchpoints, and in many ways overresearch those few. While it's true that the other touchpoints may offer less exposure or are less of an investment in marketing dollars, they are still important. We need to make sure that each touchpoint is effective, not just the high-profile and expensive ones. Besides, a little research can go a long way. We are not always talking huge research budgets. Remember to do just enough to confirm your judgment or to make sure that the experience works for the consumer.

Concentrate on the touchpoints where you have the least experience so that you can use the research data to make up for the judgment that you can't exercise. Ironically, this may be the newer, lower-profile touchpoints (like banner advertising or Twitter) rather than the more tried-and-true ones like television advertising.

It's your call based on your experience and of course the budget. At the end of the day, analytics will prove the success of the marketing. And certainly in-market sales data will be all the proof needed once the experience effect is actually in the marketplace. But a little research along the way will help get the in-market results you want.

As an example, show consumers the new website and see if they are getting the kind of information they are looking for at that touchpoint:

- Should the website be information-rich or more light and entertaining?

- What is the most important section of the website for consumers and where do they navigate to first?

- Should the website offer options for purchase, or is that not important to consumers?

- How are consumers navigating the website and where are they spending the most time?

- Are consumers able to get to the content they are searching for, or do they get frustrated and leave?

- Is the website contributing to the brand's success and serving its role in the experience effect?

For a website, there are certain metrics that research will provide to help answer some of these questions. Proprietary research will help confirm the specific decisions made while building the experience effect. And if there's uncertainty about what to do at a touchpoint, research will help us decide how best to build the brand experience. It's best to ask ourselves these kinds of questions ahead of time so that we can build the metrics into the process. The metrics are what we will measure, so it's difficult to build them into the plan after the fact. This doesn't mean that we can't, but it will save a lot of grief and rework to discuss it up front.

To continue the website example, we would ask these kinds of questions at the outset to make sure we will get the metrics we know we will need. We need to know up front that we will want to measure, for example:

- The most frequented areas of the site

- The average time spent on the site

- Click-through rate to a shopping cart

- Navigation flow into, around, and out of the website

- User satisfaction

- Number of hits and unique visitors to the site

Notice the linkage to the prior questions. The purpose for thinking this through ahead of time is to get the data we need to analyze our effectiveness, so that ultimately we can create the kind of brand experience that consumers need and want and that is unlike any other brand in the category.

The goal is to own the experience effect—with data in hand to know we are successful.

CHAPTER 13

A Flash of Color
Owning the Experience Effect .

AT THIS POINT, we are well down our development path. We know who we are as a brand, we've done our homework on our consumer targets, and we've written profiles about their lives that have allowed us to map out their daily lifestyles and identify all the places where we can connect. We've identified the touchpoints most important to the brand, we've tailored our brand messaging and communication to each touchpoint, and we've even done some research to make sure that the experience we've created is engaging at each touchpoint.

We have created the experience effect—a consistent but tailored map of experiences that becomes the brand for our consumer. But have we made it ownable? Is the experience effect our brand and uniquely our brand alone?

In theory it should be ownable. If we've done our homework we should have created a brand identity that is uniquely ours. And we should understand our consumer targets and how they connect with the brand better than anyone else in the category. So our job should be done, right? In theory, yes. But because marketing is more art than science, let's just make sure.

Let's add a few ownable elements into the brand experience. Some of the elements may feel somewhat tactical at first glance. These elements may become ownable because no other brand could possibly re-create them, and others can become ownable over time because the brand creates such a strong linkage in consumers' minds that no other brand can touch it. Although these elements seem tactical at first glance, they can become a strategic part of the brand definition. Besides, even tactics should be rooted in brand strategy, right?

Color

It can be as simple as a color. Don't brush color off as merely tactical. Color is often a core part of the brand experience. The fascinating part is that color can be central to a brand identity and brand experience without consumers consciously realizing it. It's all about the marketing. Study a few categories in the consumer packaged goods arena like skin care, hair care, laundry detergent, cereal, and soup—or for that matter even toothbrushes and razor blades. Notice that each major brand in the category tends to own a color. Store shelves literally contain dominant blocks of color in each category. When you consciously observe the packaging on the shelf, it's quite amazing. Color choice is part of a deliberate plan by marketers to create an ownable experience on at least two brand touchpoints—packaging and the retail point of purchase—and the color experience can certainly extend beyond those.

Look at the soup aisle in the grocery store and it's incredibly easy to pick out the Campbell's products because of the dominance of red and white on the shelf. Check out the Campbell's website and what dominates? The colors red and white. In the detergent aisle, pure white and powdery blue belongs to Clorox packaging. Same with the Clorox website, collateral material, and in-store displays. In hair care, Garnier Fructis owns a bright shade of green that no one else touches.

If we follow the experience effects of Campbell's, Clorox, and Garnier Fructis, we see that these brands consistently use their signature colors in the range of marketing communications as a key ingredient in the brand experiences. These brands build a consistent consumer experience at each touchpoint, rooted in the same basic brand colors. Notice the clothes that Mr. Clean from Clorox wears exclusively? White. And he purposefully has a powdery blue haze around him! It doesn't hurt that white is also the core rational benefit of the brand either.

One of the first exercises we always do when designing packaging is a color exploratory in the category. We conduct an exhaustive study of the colors being used by brands and try to link them to their brand equities. Marketers want to understand who owns specific colors in the category because it can have a tremendous impact on the consumer experience. Most of the time, we avoid using another brand's signature color because it's likely to cause confusion in the category. Using another brand's color prevents our own brand from developing a unique identity.

Imagine introducing a new soup and using red and white as the signature colors for the brand? Consumers would not recognize the brand as a new option in the soup aisle—they would automatically assume that they were looking at the Campbell's soup they know so well. Of course, the marketers of generic products are famous for following this copycat strategy. Many private-label brands intentionally do this to confuse consumers and to steal sales from the major brands in the category. Private-label marketers actually want consumers to think they're buying the market leader or at least create the perception that there is no difference between the brands. Even I have come home from shopping to find that I mistakenly bought a private-label product because it looked so incredibly similar to the brand I thought I was buying. Generic marketers are leveraging the fact that color can help own a brand experience. Clever? I suppose, if you think imitation is the sincerest form of flattery. But in terms of owning an experience effect, I say, "Get your own color!"

In terms of owning an experience effect, I say, "Get your own color!"

Go to the pain reliever aisle at any drugstore and look at both the branded products and their generic competition. It's amazing to see that each major brand owns a color and has a generic competitor that mimics it. Most consumer packaged good categories follow some of the same rules—skin care, first aid, and even food products.

Some brand colors become so ownable that just a quick flash of color in the category sparks the brand experience in consumers' minds:

- Financial services: Aqua green is American Express

- Candy: Gold is Godiva

- Laundry detergent: Orange is Tide

Susan G. Komen for the Cure is a great example in the charity space. No brand in these industries can even touch pink because marketers know that consumers will automatically, in a flash, connect the pink communication to Susan G. Komen for the Cure. The organization has done a tremendous job of linking the signature pink color to its work in the breast cancer nonprofit arena. In consumers' minds, pink has become breast cancer and Susan G. Komen for the Cure. The organization has even used its signature pink color in product design partnerships with other brands like

> *Marketers know that consumers will automatically, in a flash, connect the pink communication to Susan G. Komen for the Cure.*

KitchenAid. When we see a product that's pink, we almost automatically connect it with breast cancer and Susan G. Komen for the Cure.

The charity organization (RED) has created a similar ownership of the color red for their fund-raising efforts. Made most famous with its partnership with the Gap, the brand uses the color red in all its marketing partnerships with other great brands like iPod and American Express. (RED) owns the color red in the charity space and in many of its partner product categories now as well.

Is there some confusion with the American Heart Association and its "Go Red for Women" campaign? Perhaps. This is a good example of two brands fighting for ownership of a color in the same general category, charity. Many marketers believe that the key is to pick a unique color that no other brand owns in the category.

But no brand has used color to build a consistent brand experience better than UPS. Remember the advertising campaign, "What can brown do for you?" UPS actually took its signature brown color and consciously used it as the one defining feature of the brand experience. The color is best experienced on the trucks, but also the drivers' uniforms, shipping supplies, website, and in the UPS Store. The color brown even became the brand's advertising slogan and brand promise. What a great example this is of owning a color and using it consistently in the experience effect. When I see a brown truck coming down the street, I don't have to see the UPS logo to know that I have a delivery coming and that I can expect to see a UPS driver in a brown uniform handing me a brown envelope.

Logo

Color is not the only ownable element in our brand experience arsenal, however. Obviously, the brand logo becomes an ownable feature when done right. There are many cases where marketers rely on their logo and the design of their logo to create ownable identities and experiences from touchpoint to touchpoint:

- The red target in the Target store logo has become an iconic, pop culture symbol of smart shopping.

- The yellow arches of McDonald's instantly draw families in for a quick bite to eat.

- The arm and hammer in the Arm & Hammer logo instantly communicates purity, freshness, and strength.

Notice that these brands rarely even use the brand name anymore. Simply the iconic device of the logo (and its accompanying color) communicates the brand experience in a flash.

Target has done an incredible job of using its logo as a core part of the brand experience from touchpoint to touchpoint. It's an unmistakable element every time a consumer interacts with the brand, no matter where. Advertising, in-store, website, collateral materials, you name it. There is a huge billboard near Times Square in New York that has only the Target emblem on it repeatedly. There is not even a store nearby!

While McDonald's and Arm & Hammer also rely on their readily identifiable logos for brand recognition, I'm not sure they have aggressively used them to build a brand experience as much as

Target has. I think there's a great opportunity for these brands, or potentially for any brand, to leverage the power of their own logos. I'm sure that many could argue that McDonald's has done this to a great extent, but I don't think as much as Target has.

These are powerful brands with incredible logo recognition, but none is more famous and sought after than the Nike swoosh. The swoosh is the gold standard in logo recognition, signaling an incredible brand experience. So much so that the brand doesn't even need to use the brand name anymore. Using just the swoosh tells consumers that it's the Nike experience. Although the same can be said for Target, Nike was ahead of its time. Of course, this kind of recognition does not happen overnight. It comes after years and years of consistent marketing. As marketers we can certainly speed up the process by consistently using the logo as a core ingredient.

The Nike swoosh is the gold standard in logo recognition, signaling an incredible brand experience.

Typeface

Sometimes a brand can own an experience through an ownable typeface, believe it or not. If the brand uses the same typeface consistently over the years, it can become an ownable feature of the brand experience.

The classic example here is Coca-Cola. The brand could literally change the words in the logo, but if the typeface is the same consumers will still read it as the Coca-Cola brand logo. It's interesting to see the logos from around the world—all in different languages but with the same typeface that instantly reads as the Coca-Cola brand (of course, consistent use of the Coca-Cola red and white color scheme helps too). A typeface does not necessarily make for a brand experience unto itself, so this method of ownership for the experience effect is not as strong as color per se. But if part of the brand experience is getting consumers to readily recognize the brand and identify with it, then a consistently used, unique typeface can certainly help.

Fragrance

We've been talking about elements that consumers can see, but the other four senses can become ownable features for the brand as well, if we get really clever and innovative. Certainly for some brands, fragrance can become part of the unique experience. Personal care brands definitely use fragrance as part of their brand experience, as each brand tends to have an ownable fragrance for the product line. The magic comes when that fragrance is also leveraged across other parts of the brand experience. Think Old Spice and we all know the experience.

If the brands were clever, they would bring their unique smells to other touchpoints.

Distinctive food restaurants like Mrs. Fields and Cinnabon are other examples where visitors are immediately met with the unique smells of their signature food products. I don't know that these brands are leveraging the smells as much as they could, but it is certainly a core part of the brand experience when visiting one of their locations. If the brands were clever, then they would bring the unique smells to other touchpoints as well, such as fragranced print ads.

I know that for Starbucks, smell became an influential feature in the success of the shops when they first opened. The baristas making coffee created such a welcoming sensation of fragrance and warmth that the aroma helped to define the brand's character in the early days. I don't think Starbucks leveraged the aroma extensively, and certainly not across other touchpoints like the brand could have. What a missed opportunity, if you ask me!

I would advise brands that have the opportunity to use the sense of smell, like Mrs. Fields, Cinnabon, or Starbucks, to use that brand feature across many parts of the brand experience—not just in one touchpoint like in the retail store.

Sound

Sound can also be an ownable element that can be leveraged across all relevant touchpoints. I realize this is not easy—it's often difficult to leverage elements like smell and sound across multiple touchpoints because of the sheer executional constraints. But certainly a familiar sound can be key, particularly when it's delivered by yet another element of the brand experience and when it's consistent with the brand personality.

- Giggle: Pillsbury (the giggle perfectly matches the brand "character")

- Snap, Crackle, Pop: Kellogg's Rice Krispies (the actual sound of the product)

- Bum, bum, bum, bum: Intel ("Intel Inside" for the microprocessor inside the computer)

The NBC television network has a very ownable sound that accompanies the logo, which the brand has used to build a consistent experience, from the very early days of the network actually. It's in all the brand's advertising, certainly, and on the websites as well. There was a recent campaign that even featured the popular stars of the network humming the now famous tones. Go on a site tour at NBC and it's the first thing that the tour guide does to get everyone's attention.

Personality

Even a brand personality or attitude can be ownable, transcending all five senses. To oversimplify the point, the brand can be the whimsical personality in the category, or it can be the technical personality. Personality should be decided early in the development process, as we discussed in chapter three, when we are defining the brand.

The brand personality can indeed become an ownable element if the product actually delivers on it:

- L'Oréal: Self-worth ("You're Worth It")

- Men's Wearhouse: Self-Confidence ("You're Gonna Like the Way You Look. I Guarantee It")

- *New York Times:* Thorough, ethical ("All the News That's Fit to Print")

The brand personality can indeed become an ownable element if the product actually delivers on it.

Of course, in all these examples, the brand has to live the personality. Men's Wearhouse delivers quality clothing at affordable prices. It is consistent. The *New York Times,* however, has had alleged lapses in its ethical reputation, which puts its stated personality into question.

When thinking about brand attitude, Kenneth Cole comes to mind. Kenneth Cole is the sassy, politically charged brand in fashion. The brand's clever advertising quips and timely pop culture relevance have become famous in marketing circles. The sassy attitude of Kenneth Cole has been consistent for years, in many of the brand's marketing channels. When the economy suffered a big downturn, the headline statement on the Kenneth Cole website said, "Make the Most of Wearing Times." To support an AIDS walk in Los Angeles, the brand ran a print ad that said, "Join the Party . . . Be an Accessory." Kenneth Cole owns this attitude in the fashion business and no other brand has been able to touch it. This is the experience effect at work, based solely on a personality and attitude.

Many other brands use a personality or an attitude to create a brand experience. Just look at any brand that uses a spokesperson. That brand is leveraging the personality of that spokesperson onto the brand itself, hoping that consumers will experience the brand in the same way they experience the spokesperson. William Shatner for Priceline.com is a great example. As consumers, we completely associate the personality of William Shatner with the personality of the brand he represents, Priceline.com. The interesting part is that because the advertising mimics the personality of William Shatner, the brand now has that personality as well.

Mickey Mouse for Disney is perhaps the first big example ever created. Mickey Mouse and his distinctive silhouette embody the spirit of Disney and defined the brand at its inception. Of course Walt Disney himself was a big piece of it at the time as well. The Disney brand has evolved and grown tremendously since those days, but notice that the brand uses the personality and attitude of all its characters, including Mickey Mouse, to keep its brand experience alive.

* * *

Many of these techniques, as I mentioned, appear to be tactical. Colors, typefaces, smells, and sounds are all tactical elements in marketing execution, or so they seem. Even an attitude can appear to be executional in nature.

Don't save these elements for last though, because they should be part of the strategic process we've been talking about all along. Plan these elements ahead of time as a part of the strategic building of the experience effect, as part of the very essence of the brand definition.

Like the colors for the brand, for example. Select colors that make strategic sense for the brand definition and for consumer needs and wants. Conduct a color exploratory in the category as I mentioned. Pick colors that make sense for the brand and that no other brand owns.

Years ago green was not a good choice for a food brand because it symbolized mold and staleness in consumers' minds. Believe it or not, food brands stayed away from green for very strategic reasons back in the day. At the time, consumer research even proved that green left an impression of mold. Then along came Healthy Choice, using a very prominent green for its packaging! Suddenly green meant delicious, fresh, and healthy. The brand embraced the color and changed perceptions. Now Healthy Choice owns green in the frozen food section of grocery stores and in consumers' minds as fresh, healthy food. No other food brand in the category can touch the color green. What appears to be a tactical execution of the packaging was actually a strategic decision that Healthy Choice made up front in the brand development process. As a result, it not only changed consumer perceptions but also created an ownable experience with packaging that it has consistently used in other touchpoints as well.

Of course, the more strategically based the brand ownership, the better. Although color is a great tool, competitors can easily copy it.

Let's explore some other strategic ways to own a specific brand experience that are perhaps a little harder for a competitor to combat.

Claims

This is the stuff for which patents and other forms of legal and regulatory protection are made. If there's a unique claim for the product that no one else can make, then use it as the basis for an ownable brand proposition and experience.

Pharmaceutical and some over-the-counter healthcare products often enjoy this strategic advantage as the first in a category to claim to treat a disease or lessen the severity of a symptom. They make every attempt to own it in their marketing.

Claims are not just for drugs though. Verizon Wireless is perhaps a good example of using a claim about network coverage across the experience effect. The brand appears to make a network coverage claim that no other brand can make, or it has at least spun it in a way that sounds unique. Sometimes the creative spin can itself become ownable, which is the case with Verizon Wireless. The brand has done a good job of using a seemingly unique claim of network coverage consistently across its marketing elements.

If there is a unique claim, absolutely use it throughout the experience effect. A claim to do something that consumers need and that no one else can claim is marketing gold!

Innovation

An innovation in the product or its packaging can also become an ownable consumer experience for a brand. The question is always how long it will be unique before another brand picks it up.

Patents protect, but only for some, and only for so long! But while you have it, use it and build an experience around it for the maximum impact.

The stand-up toothpaste tube is a good example of a packaging innovation that was unique at first, but only for a short time until every other brand copied it. In the marketing world, owning the stand-up toothpaste tube lasted about a minute, but it was indeed an innovative and unique experience while it lasted.

The iPod is the standout here: iPod has done an incredible job leveraging its continual innovation in technology, product design, and packaging. The iPod experience effect is completely built around the design and functionality of this little device that changed the music industry, pop culture, and entire facets of consumers' lives. The iPod brand experience carries right into the Apple stores, truly an experience effect if you have ever visited one. The store is loaded with large, welcoming tables that spaciously feature the merchandise. All the latest products are ready to be touched, picked up, and demonstrated. The store is organized by product type, so you can quickly go to the iPods or to the laptops or to the desktops. Upstairs, classes and repairs are conveniently offered and scheduled to maximize your own usage of the products. A total experience, and it is all Apple with the iPod on the center stage. Not to mention the bold print and online advertising that deliver this experience as well.

While others have tried to copy it, no other brand has come close to the experience effect of the iPod. Of course it was the first brand with an mp3 player that could hold an entire collection of CDs, and once video was possible, the brand became unstoppable. The iPod's innovations have been continuous, which is also a part of the brand experience. As I mentioned, these more strategically based distinguishing features, like product innovation, are much harder to come by but generally easier for a brand to keep. And if it's truly unique and meaningful, make it central to the experience effect.

*   *   *

For most brands, we just have to work harder to own the experience effect. Let consumers be the guide, and create a meaningful experience for them. If we've defined the brand thoroughly and if the brand is rooted in the lifestyle of the consumer targets—all their wants, needs, desires, and behaviors—then by design the experience effect is ownable.

The secret ingredient to an ownable experience effect is to have the best, deepest, most strategically based connection with the consumer that a brand can possibly have. Do it better than anyone else and it will be completely ownable. Just in case, add a flash of color.

Now let's find out if anything is missing.

> *The secret ingredient to an ownable experience effect is to have the best, deepest, most strategically based connection with the consumer that a brand can possibly have.*

CHAPTER **14**

Mind the Gap

Assessing What's Missing on the Brand

WE'VE WALKED THROUGH all the essential building blocks of the experience effect and we've even described how we can make sure we own it. It's time to get to work.

Those who are launching a brand for the first time will be facing very different challenges than those with an established brand. For a new brand that is just about to hit the marketplace, in some ways it is easier to build the experience effect than for an established brand, and in some ways it is much harder.

For new brands, the best part is starting from scratch. There are no preconceived notions about what's right and what's wrong, or at least not as many. And there are not as many voices pointing out what's already been done and what can't possibly work.

This makes a marketer's job much easier in some ways. When starting from scratch, there's a clean slate. No baggage, less drama, and fewer arbitrary rules. A marketer's dream, some might say. For a new brand, simply start from the beginning of the process and step through it as we've been outlining, beginning with defining the brand.

While I won't pretend that this book is the be-all and end-all for marketers, the experience effect process that we've been discussing will get a new brand to a pretty good place. At least that's the goal—whether the brand is a new consumer packaged good, retail store, clothing line, restaurant, or even a small business.

When everything is new, we have to define the brand, understand the consumer, and map out the touchpoints.

Keep in mind that starting fresh means that everything must be done for the first time, and that's no small task. Nothing exists, so everything has to be created, along every single touchpoint. And there might not be much existing research to help skip a step or two. When everything is new, we have to define the brand, understand the consumer, and map out the touchpoints. We need to unfold the entire process, which is a lot of work.

When managing an existing brand, however, at least some of that work is done or is in progress. Depending on how long the brand has been around, there may be years of consumer research studies, brand tracking results, and marketing analyses that can provide a brand manager with a huge head start. There's no benefit of a clean slate, of course, but a history of market results can certainly advance the process.

Having said all this, beginning the process is more or less the same regardless of the brand's tenure. We need to outline our goals in either scenario. What are we trying to accomplish? We need to create a quick list of what we want the experience effect to do. This is the best way to start.

For a new brand, are you trying to innovate and steal market share from a vulnerable leader within your category? For an established brand, are you trying to update the offerings and keep the brand contemporary? Or does the brand need a wholesale reinvention to stay current? I've learned that the best way to start anything is to outline the goals. We can't get started unless we know what we are trying to do.

Keep the goals simple so we'll know when we've reached them. If it is overly complicated, we'll spend all our time writing goals and no time actually attaining them! Commit the goals to paper and make them real for greater clarity.

We often forget to state our goals up front, which I believe is half the battle. We dive right in and start solving, before we even know what we are solving for. We start acting before we know why. I've seen it all too often. Even in business meetings, I find that team members often forget to communicate up front the goals of the meeting. To be efficient and productive, in meetings or in developing marketing programs, start everything with the goals. Then everyone involved will know where the process should end up, and they will know why they are working so hard.

Once we outline the goals, it's time for an assessment of the brand and its touchpoints. How far from the goals is the brand right now? Are we talking little tweaks or are we heading toward a whole new approach?

Goals must be clear and simple if we want to accomplish them. Some examples could include:

- Be the market leader in the segment

- Attract a new consumer target market

- Stem share losses

- Build brand awareness and household penetration

- Increase marketing return on investment (ROI)

- Revitalize engagement on the website to drive online sales

Of course, real goals should be much more specific and measurable, but this serves as a helpful example. If the goal is to increase marketing ROI, then simply state the actual numbers targeted and the time frame, for instance. That way the entire team will know when the brand has reached the goal.

If the goals are broad, like many of the ones above, then you may need to break them down into subgoals. But don't overcomplicate. Keep it simple and get to the real work! Once we have the goals committed to paper and to the rest of the team, we can start the process of building the experience effect.

A gap assessment will help plan out the next steps. Gap assessments are an easy way to detail the amount of work in front of us by providing a quick glance at the road ahead, telling us how far from the completed process we currently sit. A gap assessment is similar to the needs assessment that we spoke about in chapter twelve, where we explored researching the experience effect. A gap assessment will help figure out not only how we measure up to the goals, but also how much of the experience effect we have already built. Particularly with an established brand, a gap assessment will tell us where to focus our efforts, and it will tell us what has already been completed. We can then put together the plan to accomplish what needs to get done.

Don't spend all your time on the gap assessment; get going on the real meat!

Make it quick and easy. Don't spend all your time on the gap assessment; get going on the real meat! In doing a gap assessment, simply ask yourself some key questions and jot down some notes. Follow the development process we've been outlining and list what you may have already completed:

- Brand definition:
  - How well is the brand defined?
  - Is it unique to the marketplace?
  - Have you built a perceptual map to guide the process?
  - Could another perceptual map with different dimensions help to define the brand even further?
- Consumer profiles:
  - Is there a good understanding of the consumer targets?
  - What more could be known about the consumer? How can you learn more?
  - Are there other consumer targets that could be explored?
  - Do you have consumer profiles to bring all the information together in a real way?
  - Can the profiles go deeper and become even more insightful?
- Touchpoint maps:
  - How well are the touchpoints mapped out?
  - Is there a touchpoint map for each target market?
  - Are there even more touchpoints that have not been explored?

- Are the touchpoints prioritized in importance to the target markets?

- Have the touchpoints been tailored and optimized?

- Touchpoint research:

  - Are the touchpoints accomplishing the goals set out for them?

  - Will more research help you know for sure?

- Budget:

  - What is the marketing budget?

  - Has the budget been prioritized and allocated to the touchpoints?

- Timing:

  - When is the next phase of the experience effect going to market?

  - What market pressures are influencing timing?

  - Is there a window of opportunity that the brand must meet?

The list can obviously go on and on, so this is just a representative sampling. Create a list that makes sense for the marketing challenges the brand faces. Keep the list short—maybe a dozen questions. The point here is to prioritize the goals and identify what's still left to do.

We spoke briefly about the Gap brand in chapter four, when we explored the first step in developing the experience effect, defining the brand. I think that if the Gap brand were to do a gap assessment, the brand managers would find that they need to answer more questions about how they define the brand and more questions about defining their target consumer. Doing a gap assessment would help the Gap brand to focus on what's missing in the marketing plan and would help the brand to address key business issues.

When answering some of these key questions, put the information in a grid and allocate a score from one to five (from lowest to highest) to each attribute, and then list a simple action plan for how to address the gap, as in figure 14.1. This will identify areas where resources need to be concentrated.

Compare this grid to the notes, and there will be a clear path to the critical steps in building the experience effect. It is very simple, and I like keeping things simple because it forces clarity and doesn't bog us down.

For example, if you give the brand a five on brand definition but a two on consumer profiles, then spend some time learning more about the consumer and developing really deep profiles to help build the brand experience. If you give the brand a four on touchpoint priorities but a two on measuring their effectiveness, that should tell you something too. You need to do some research to make sure the touchpoint experiences are engaging.

Once there's a brand score for each area, prioritize where to concentrate efforts. Take a look at the notes and list an action plan for each gap. Simply list some projects that the team can tackle to help move the score up toward a five. Update the grid each time you do an assessment to track the progress at key intervals in the development process.

Here's a hypothetical gap assessment for the new furniture brand we created in chapter five. Let's imagine we just picked up the brand from the brand manager before us and need to finish developing the experience effect before we launch in six months. Time is of the essence because we know another competitor is coming out in a year, and we want to beat them to the market.

Our gap assessment might look like figure 14.2.

FIGURE 14.1 Gap Assessement (Score 1–5)

Draft Date: x/x/xx

Goals: To grow market share x points in twelve months.
To improve ROI by x points in six months.

	Last Score	This Score	Action Plan
Brand Definition		5	
Consumer Profile		2	Focus on learning more about the consumer
Touchpoint Map		4	
Touchpoint Research		2	Make sure that experience created at each touchpoint is effective
Ownability			
Timetable Identified			
Budget Allocated			

FIGURE 14.2   Furniture Brand Gap Assessement (Score 1–5)

Draft Date: x/x/xx

Goals: To complete the brand launch by year's end.
To achieve an 8 percent market share within first twelve months.
To realize a 14 percent gross margin within first twelve months.

	Last Score	This Score	Action Plan
Brand Definition	3	4	Monitor competition to ensure unique space in category
Consumer Profile	3	3	Do more grassroots research to gain understanding and conduct quantitative concept testing
Touchpoint Map	1	2	Need to prioritize possible brand touchpoints and tailor experiences
Ownability	2	2	Investigate ways to add ownable elements to brand experiences
Timetable Identified	5	4	Now that launch is getting closer, keep on top of key items to complete
Budget Allocated	4	3	Continue to properly allocate remaining budget

With this gap assessment in hand, we now know where to pick up the work so that we can accomplish our goals. We know our weak spots and we've got our priorities. An action plan has been developed and we separately have a few notes as backup to the gap assessment. We can also see how we have progressed since the last time we did the assessment.

The gap assessment should be an ongoing, dynamic guide to keep you and the team on your toes.

All through the process, use the gap assessment to help keep track of the team's progress. Move items up from a score of one to three to five as the team works through the development process. Change the ratings as projects are completed so that you know where to stay focused. Over time you will close the gaps as you broaden the depth of your own marketing knowledge. As the marketplace changes and new challenges arise, new gaps will form. There will always be new items to develop—a marketer's job is never done. That's why the gap assessment should be an ongoing, dynamic guide to keep you and the team on your toes.

Chances are you are not in this alone. Marketing is a team sport, so keep your teammates in the loop as you progress.

CHAPTER **15**

A Room with a View
Keeping the Team on Track

WHEN IT COMES TO marketing and developing the experience effect for a brand, none of us are in it alone. Almost all of us work in teams, and those teams generally include colleagues, bosses, employees, associates, contractors, and suppliers. Even if you are a sole proprietor, you certainly work with suppliers, accountants, and other experts to help you with your business.

We've been observing consumers and looking at marketing examples together throughout the entire book. Great marketing comes from teams of people working together to create and execute a solid plan. We each contribute our own individual talents, but collectively we make the brand successful. A well-coordinated team can help make sure that the brand has sufficient resources and skill sets to be successful.

If we think about the process we've just outlined, there are many areas where we could potentially miss our goals and need to adjust our plan.

While teamwork can certainly be rewarding, it opens up areas of inefficiency as well. We've all seen it—the inefficient meetings, duplication of effort, and misalignment on key issues, to name a few. Like anything, when it comes to individual performance, team dynamics, and human nature, there are many things that can get in the way of our good work. Even the best of intentions can cause imperfect results. It's just the way life works.

As brand managers and brand advocates, it's our job to make sure that nothing gets in our way. It's our job to keep the entire team focused on the job at hand and to develop the most successful experience effect possible. Even when everything appears to be developing smoothly, imperfections can still sneak up on the team. We may think that we've done the best job possible, yet we still miss our goals.

If we think about the process we've just outlined, there are many areas where we could potentially miss our goals and need to adjust our plan, including:

- Competing in a far too cluttered space in the category: We might need the team to create a more distinct brand definition, as we talked about in chapter three. Perhaps the team needs to go back to the drawing board.

- Having only a cursory understanding of the consumer that is frankly not deep enough: We might need the team to do more consumer research, as we talked about in chapters four and five. Perhaps we need the team to go deeper.

- Using a fact-based approach to communicating brand benefits: We may need the team to make a more emotional connection with the consumer, as we talked about in chapter six. This is a common one. Perhaps we need to convince the team that the emotional dimension will offer a deeper connection.

- Developing inconsistent branding and inconsistent experiences from touchpoint to touchpoint: We may need the team to better connect the brand experience to the brand definition at each touchpoint, not just at a few of them, as we talked about in chapter seven. Perhaps the team has not put enough effort into each of the touchpoints.

- Not maximizing touchpoints to their best use: We may need to better understand the dynamics of the touchpoint, as we talked about in chapter eight. Perhaps the team understands some touchpoints better than others.

- Creating cookie cutter experiences from touchpoint to touchpoint: We may need to better adapt or tailor the experience to the specific touchpoint itself, as we talked about in chapter nine. Perhaps the team is taking the easy way out to save resources.

- Relying too much on our judgment in developing the experience at a touchpoint: We may need to do more research to make sure the touchpoint is being used effectively, as we talked about in chapter twelve. Perhaps some of the team members need to be convinced of the value of research, or perhaps the timetable needs to be shifted to accommodate a research phase at key touchpoints.

- Watching competitors easily copy elements of the brand experience: We may need more ownable branding elements, as we talked about in chapter thirteen. Perhaps the team needs to get more creative.

As we've discussed, we see examples of these marketing imperfections all the time, and it's not always because the marketers didn't do their jobs. Quite the contrary, they have probably been working very hard and trying to do good work. Marketing is an imperfect science and a subjective art. Anytime there is a team of people involved, there are going to be errors and disagreements.

Working with clients through the years, I've seen it over and over again, and I've noticed some common traits. All of us, from time to time, suffer from:

- Being way too busy with too many priorities and finding it hard to get everything done every day. Sad to say, some things just end up at the end of our project list. And as staffing gets cut and our teams get leaner and leaner, this becomes an even bigger issue.

- Not developing all touchpoints to the fullest extent possible. We tend to focus on the higher-priority touchpoints, like television advertising or the website, leaving the other touchpoints with fewer resources and less development time. The truth is that sometimes the less important components may need more development work because we are less familiar with them. When we have less experience with a touchpoint, we may need more resources, more time, and further research to make sure we are on the right track.

- Not connecting all the team members together and not keeping them in the loop. Because marketing work is so subjective, the brand can fall victim to a range of interpretations by various team members. This makes it hard to keep the brand experience consistent from touchpoint to touchpoint when there are different definitions of the brand and the consumer.

- Utilizing a suboptimal brand definition and consumer understanding to guide the process. This is perhaps the most common flaw, and also the most obvious. If the marketing team does not have a clear understanding of the brand and its consumer, then the experience effect cannot possibly be maximized. It's vitally important that we do our homework and share it with the team.

Theoretically, you can avoid many of these common marketing problems with a few simple techniques. We talked about some of them briefly in chapter eight, but I'd like to explore them more now and offer a few suggestions.

A simple thing like a style guide can help tremendously. If you are managing a brand right now and don't have a style guide, then I would suggest that this be the first thing you do tomorrow when you go to work. Really, do it tomorrow. When something is committed to writing in a style guide, it's amazing how it can become an integral part of the brand team. A style guide is an invaluable tool for sharing information about the brand with team members. And it also helps build consistency from touchpoint to touchpoint.

A style guide helps build consistency from touchpoint to touchpoint.

Create a style guide that documents all the relevant facets of the brand and distribute it liberally. The style guide can house all the elements of the experience effect to help create consistency both strategically and tactically among all team members and across all marketing elements. The style guide is full of useful information that will help any member of the brand team stay consistent with the brand experience. Typical items include:

- Brand definition statement. Some marketers call these brand mission statements, brand footprints, brand platforms, or brand guideposts. Call it whatever you want, just include it in the style guide! We explored defining the brand in chapter three. Include the celebrity photographs and brand soundtrack to make it more meaningful.

- Perceptual maps. Include a concise portrayal of how the brand fits in the category, whether through a perceptual map as we discussed in chapter three or through another method.

- Consumer profiles. Having current consumer profiles, a few per target market, can help the entire team keep the consumer at the forefront of their minds as they develop marketing programs. We wrote consumer profiles in chapter five.

- Logos in various sizes and formats, both in color and in black and white. This is the simple stuff that can ensure consistent branding across all communications. You'd be amazed how often logos and logo formats change, so keep this updated so that everyone on the team has access to the latest and greatest of the brand.

- Brand colors, both primary and secondary. If the brand owns a color scheme in the category, then make sure that everyone on the team has access to the official colors and uses them in their work. A brand can't own a color if it's not used consistently.

- Brand marketing assets such as photography, product demos, illustrations, package shots, video footage, etc. One of the keys to a consistent experience is using consistent brand imagery and communications. Make these brand assets available to everyone on the team via the style guide.

- Approved claims and other approved copy. It sounds unbelievable, but I've seen a lot of team members waste valuable time because they don't know where to find approved claims and approved language for the brand. These items include legally approved product claims, copyright lines, terms of usage, benefit statements, product instructions, etc. The style guide is a great place to house this vitally important information once it's been approved by legal counsel and management.

- Required formats like spec sheets for key marketing items. How the brand identity or the current marketing campaign translates into marketing communications should be monitored and supervised. Having spec sheets for key items will certainly help in the process by eliminating some of the technical issues in implementation.

- Current in-market campaign communications with copies of all elements across the touchpoints. This is where sharing really kicks in. Placing all the current marketing communications into the style guide allows everyone to see what other teammates are creating. This will not only guide their work, but also help each person see how his or her work fits in the context of the entire brand.

The style guide should be a rich asset for the entire team, to make sure that everyone is on the same page, so to speak. I've listed some ideas for inclusion, but put anything in there that will keep the team connected, focused, and consistent. Make it ownable unto itself.

Make sure the style guide is a living, breathing document that everyone on the brand can use.

Once the style guide is created, share it with anyone who touches the brand. Publish it for the team, either online or in a book. Make sure it's a living, breathing document that everyone on the brand can use. Update the style guide from time to time, ideally once a year if not more often. There is nothing worse than a style guide that is outdated. Generally speaking, electronic formats are easier to keep updated. It will be a lot less work and a lot less money to update it each time.

I would suggest a quarterly team update or status meeting. Include everyone who touches the brand, not just the folks who frequent the brand the most. Peripheral teammates can add a lot of value when put in the right forum—they can often provide a more objective point of view because they are not as close to the business.

This is the perfect time to present the gap assessment that we spoke about in chapter fourteen. Allow the entire team to comment on the missing elements and to update the team on progress made to date.

Continually monitor the progress of the team against the goals and against the plan for the experience effect. Make sure everything is progressing, both strategically for the brand as well as executionally. Timetable tracking and budget management are critical to keeping the team together. Update the gap assessment and distribute it to the team so that everyone is engaged and in the loop.

Many brand managers create a common space at the office where all the brand communication elements are posted in one place for everyone on the brand to observe, participate in, and comment on. These common areas are often called war rooms, and the ultimate goal is consistency in the marketplace. A war room can be a place where the team can stay connected and keep in touch with each other on different aspects of the brand and where teammates can get a view of the entire brand experience. Of course, remember that the war room can be physical, virtual, or both. Just make it accessible and current. Check out a few software programs that can easily be distributed to create a virtual war room—a virtual room with a virtual view for the team!

The war room can also be used as a tool in the approval process. It's important for members of the marketing team to approve each other's work so that consistency and tailoring can be easily monitored. The war room is a place to send team members, including senior management, to review and approve the work. With any team, make sure that work is being shared and that senior management is in the loop. The war room will help, but it won't completely replace a more formal approval process to keep the work flowing.

An approval process also allows more junior members of the team to get the experience of managing projects while being supervised and guided by the more senior members. It's wonderful for more junior team members to get the opportunity to manage key projects, but always with a safety net. A rigorously followed process takes away some of the risk so that the more senior members of the team have a chance to review the work before it hits the marketplace, ensuring that it fits the planned brand experience. The process also ensures that the more junior team members are working consistently with the brand.

Let more junior team members manage key projects—but always with a safety net.

The pitfalls that large national brands face are often no different from those of the smaller brands. It's generally just a matter of scale and scope. Even if the brand is a small business like a restaurant or a retail store, the experience effect process is largely the same, and the problems marketers face tend to be similar. There are still multiple people on the team, even if they are outside vendors or family members. The brand still relies on them for different elements of the plan and still needs them to keep consistency among touchpoints. Simplified versions of the suggestions we have discussed will help even a small-business owner or a brand manager of a small brand. For example, there's no need for an elaborate style guide when a comprehensive page or two will do wonders for the brand marketing plan.

Most important, don't get frustrated or overwhelmed. There's always an opportunity to improve our work. Even when the process is finished, we have to begin thinking about how to update and evolve it. If the marketplace changes or competitors are on the top of their game, then the brand has to be dynamic in its marketing too. Even if things are running smoothly, something always comes along to disrupt it. A marketer's job is never done.

Work to continually evolve the brand, keep it relevant, and keep it unique. Consumer needs change, and of course the marketplace changes all the time. Work to make the consumer profiles deeper, and add more target consumers to build the business when appropriate. New touchpoints come along in the market- place, so see if they make sense for the consumer, especially now in digital marketing and social media.

Every year, if not more often, update the gap assessment on the brand and do more research on the experience effect to keep it alive and successfully working. Update the style guide to keep it current, and keep sharing it with the team. The brand experience will be all the richer.

Click-Through
Making It Real

READING ABOUT GOOD MARKETING is just one step in *The Experience Effect* journey. Applying what you've read to a real brand or marketing challenge is where the actual work begins.

I've read a lot of marketing and business books, and I'm sure you have as well. To be quite honest, I tend to react to them with mixed emotions. On the one hand, almost all of them have been interesting in one way or another, and I always manage to take away a new nugget or two to help me in my job. I have found every book to be at least a little thought-provoking on some level, even if merely to resurrect principles I have not thought about in a long time. At the same time, though, I find most marketing books to be far too theoretical. I really do struggle sometimes to apply the principles I am reading to my own marketing challenges.

What usually happens is that I finish the book quickly, put it up on my shelf with a collection of other business books, and hurry on to the real-time marketing challenges of the day. Yes, that is the exact point; I quickly move on to these challenges and forget what I've just read.

My goal at the outset of this book was to offer practical, real-life advice to help you be a better marketer. I promised not to be too theoretical and not to use too many buzzwords. I wanted the book to be simple and pragmatic. I've tried to make this book enjoyable to read, not too technical, and certainly applicable to your own business.

My attempt was to mix marketing concepts with real examples, so remember to heed the lessons learned from all the brands that we looked at: from Starbucks to Nike, from Gap to Louis Vuitton, from Verizon to Keebler, and from Jessica Simpson to Dolly Parton. And don't forget the inspirational The Biggest Loser, the entertainment property that is quickly becoming a classic brand.

Now turn your investment time of reading this book into a practical start to a more effective marketing plan for your brand. Use the tools and concepts you've read about to continually evolve your brand's experience effect over time. Please keep in mind that the process I outlined here cannot possibly be totally inclusive of what it takes to do great marketing. You will absolutely need to weave these concepts in with the work that you already do for your brand and with any company policies that exist. But I do hope that I've given you a way of thinking that can supplement your current efforts and can help you do a better job.

As you work through the challenges on your brand, be sure to visit me at JimJosephExp.com. Ask me some hard questions and I'll try to give some more sound advice. Join discussions with other readers who are looking to solve their marketing challenges too. Let's keep the experience alive.

Best of luck to you. It's been an experience! Jim.

Index

About the Author

JIM JOSEPH is an award-winning, veteran marketing professional who specializes in building consumer brands and agency businesses. Jim's consistent goal throughout his career has been to help blockbuster clients including Kellogg's, Kraft, Cadillac, Tylenol, Clean & Clear, Aveeno, Durex, AFLAC, Ambien CR, and Wal-Mart create successful brand experiences that engage consumers and add value to their lives.

Currently President and Partner of Lippe Taylor Brand Communications in New York City, Jim has spent the bulk of his agency career at Publicis Groupe, where he started his own agency. Jim then merged his boutique firm with two others to create Arc-NY, the largest integrated marketing services agency in Manhattan at the time. Jim later took over as head of Saatchi & Saatchi Wellness, where he successfully transformed the agency's strategy from traditional advertising to diversified marketing. During his tenure, the agency won several prestigious industry awards, including "Agency of the Year" from DTC Perspectives on Excellence, "Most Creative Agency" from The Manny Awards, and a Grand CLIO for advertising.

Early in his career on the client side at Johnson & Johnson, Jim became a new products expert by launching nine new consumer products in less than five years—including the number-one Reach Wondergrip toothbrush for kids and the reinvention of Clean & Clear skin care for teenage girls. Jim then went on to be the lead marketer for the Arm & Hammer Dental Care toothpaste line.

A sought-after speaker, Jim is a graduate of Cornell University and has an MBA from Columbia University. He lives in Manhattan and Bucks County, Pennsylvania, with his partner of more than ten years and his two teenage children. When not working with his team or spending time with his family, Jim is likely to be found running along the Hudson River or writing his blog at JimJosephExp.com.